# Hope from the City

John Vincent

# Hope from the City

EPWORTH PRESS

0 7162 0533 5


*Author's royalties are to be donated to the Urban
Theology Unit,
210 Abbeyfield Road, Sheffield S4 7AZ*


First published 2000
by Epworth Press
20 Ivatt Way
Peterborough, PE3 7PG

Typeset by Regent Typesetting, London
Printed and bound in Great Britain by
Biddles Ltd, Guildford and King's Lynn

*This book is dedicated to
colleagues and co-workers in the
Sheffield Inner City Ecumenical Mission
with much affection and gratitude for thirty years'
common pilgrimage and learning,*

*with special thanks to
Iain and Janette Cloke, Jane Grinonneau, Ian Lucraft,
Barry Swift, and Grace Vincent who critiqued
and improved it,
and to Anne Lewis and Janet Colby who put it all
on computer disk.*

# Contents

## PART THREE

### DRINKING FROM OUR OWN WELLS

*Spiritualities and Strategies for Christians and Churches*

PART FOUR

HOPES AND PROSPECTS

*Hearing It Again for the Future of Our Cities*

# Foreword

More than twenty-five years ago I contributed to a community magazine called *Pitsmoor News*. I joined with local residents like John Vincent in combating 'the Authority knows best' attitude to bulldozing the housing and indulging in the wholesale demolition of a community. I backed what in those days was called community leadership – and which nowadays is known as capacity building.

As this book rightly says, the seeds fall on very different ground and some sprout in abundance, sometimes to flourish and die quickly, sometimes to take hold and yield much fruit.

Back in the early 1930s, R. H. Tawney referred to the very different ways in which adult education and community learning could express itself. Now today, as this book illustrates, the melting pot of cultural diversity and religious and social influences will form fertile ground for radical ideas, for a challenge to the establishment and for improvement built from the very roots of the community.

We have now moved from the church's report *Faith in the City*, through to this reflection of *Hope from the City*. This hope is crucial because, in the end, only by ensuring that those who themselves live in the most deprived communities have the capacity to generate ideas and rally the strength needed to find answers to their problems, can we really build a different society.

Of course, government will be crucial to providing the resources and the frameworks which enable people to develop their own solutions. But, as this book indicates, the interchange of individual and community commitment with outside influences, including the crucial role of those whose faith drives them to give their lives to others, can make the crucial difference.

In the end, as has so often been proved, even substantial investment in bricks and mortar will come to nothing unless the seed has taken root. Only if the community itself has the ability to be able to grow, to respond, and to take control of circumstance, will it be possible to succeed.

Now, twenty-five years on, as a member of the Cabinet, I still reflect on those lessons, and I still believe that in the end democracy should rest on the decision-making of those for whom it is intended, and not solely on the well-meaning benevolence of those who legislate from on high.

David Blunkett
*Secretary of State for Education and Employment*
*MP for Sheffield Brightside*

# Preface

*Hope from the City* deals with the issues of our contemporary urban scene, from the standpoint of a group of inner city and housing estate communities. My fundamental argument is that if we listened to the people, the situations, and the experiences of areas like these, we would see the problems of cities in their true light, and recognize where elements of hope for the future really are.

Three kinds of people are my intended readers.

First, the politicians, national and local. Many policies of government, old Tory or new Labour, old welfare or politically correct, do not actually deliver, down here in the inner city. So, this book is a plea for some radical re-orientations in urban policy, inviting politicians even to learn from simple people inspired by old Bible stories!

Second, the ordinary concerned reader. I believe the current 'me and my' culture is basically an insult to human beings. So, this book is an argument for a new self-commitment and even heroism, based on the alternative journey of intentional Christian discipleship, following the hints of people actually doing it today, and a renewed biblical interpretation and theology, which I shall elaborate in more detail in a forth-coming companion volume, *Theology from the City*.

Third, the churches. Nearly three years on from *The Cities* Report, the denominations are actually cutting back on their urban support. So, this book argues for new policies, based on 'bottom-up' communities and projects, and for a preparedness to listen to some different models for church and mission.

The book also salutes and hopefully assists my colleague,

Inderjit Bhogal, in his year from June 2000 as President of the Methodist Conference. Here are his people, his places, and some of his concerns.

John Vincent
*February 2000*

# PART ONE

# THE DYNAMICS OF CHANGE

*Getting it Together in the Inner City*

*Yours the city, yours the city,*
*With no place to lay your head.*
*Yours the courage, yours the pity,*
*Yours the life among the dead.*
*Yours the poor, and yours the beaten,*
*Struggling to reclaim their rights.*
*Yours the victimized we threaten,*
*Seeking allies for their fights.*

*Yours the claimant, yours the homeless,*
*Unemployed and underpaid.*
*Yours the children, desperate, powerless,*
*Yours the bleeding heart betrayed.*
*Yours the hopes by cities heightened,*
*Rastas, pop groups, youth in quest.*
*Yours the rich, though unenlightened*
*By the poor you make the blest.*

*Yours the movement for empowering,*
*Yours the kingdom, sure and meek,*
*Yours the banquet for our flowering,*
*Yours the shalom cities seek.*
*Ours your faithful love upholding,*
*Ours your grace outpassing fears,*
*Ours the mystery unfolding*
*Christ who wipes away all tears.*

John Vincent

# I

# Seeds in the City

Seeds in the city?

In our inner city street, seeds get everywhere, unwanted and unplanned. The streets are littered with grass and weeds growing in the cracks of concrete, or the edges of footpaths, or in the neglected parks and cemetery. Their growth is disorganized, chaotic, wild, and harbours dirt and rubbish. They are one more eyesore, one more sign of the absence of street cleaners, community gardeners, or locals who care for the environment.

Yet the seeds in the streets are signs of hope. They are signs of life in the concrete city, sprouts of defiance against imposed tarmac, an ecological return to nature in a cold, technological, constructed environment. They hold the promise that the future could be wholesome, humane and satisfying.

Very few seeds are sown intentionally. A few gardens which are loved and cared for are the exception. Window boxes and hanging baskets transform a street, but are not often there. Those who venture them have courage against the neglect all around. Plants which are grown intentionally are often wrenched out by tiny hands, or the heads of flowers cut off by youngsters unaccustomed to growing things. There was a spate of thefts of planted flowers this last spring.

Seeds in the city? Yes. I want to suggest that the image of seeds is a way into understanding our stories and gives us clues to our message to the rest of the world!

Seeds are a prominent feature in Jesus' parables. He sees the seed's activity as a sign, even an example of God's happening, God's realm, God's Kingdom. The most significant parable for us is the well-known parable of the sower which begins in Mark

4. 2–3, where Jesus, talking to his listeners, points to a poor peasant smallholder, sowing his seed on the not very good earth which is all he is allowed to work on:

> Jesus taught them many things in parables,
> And when he was teaching, he said
>> 'Listen to this!
>> Look over there,
>> Look at the sower going out to sow.'

The rest of the parable describes four different kinds of soil or earth into which the seeds fall, producing different results. We will take them one by one.

> It happened, that as he sowed,
> Some seeds fell on the path,
> But then came the birds
> And swallowed them up (v. 4).

The first kind of situation into which the seeds have fallen is not at all propitious. Taking the four different soils we can estimate that 25% simply fall on the footpath, where the birds immediately see them, and swallow them up. So, in our stories, perhaps 25% of what we do is just bits of bread for people in need. Like the birds, they gobble them up, and go off looking for the next bits of help somewhere else. And that is fine. The hungry must be fed. There are many hungry in the city. And there must always be places, projects and people for them. We have to be there, as much as we can, for those in need. As John Wesley says, we must 'Go not only to those who need you, but to those who need you most.'

> Other seeds fell in rocky ground,
> Where they did not have much soil,
> And they sprang up quickly,
> But because they had no depth of soil
> When the sun came out,

They were scorched
And, having no root, withered away (vv. 5–6).

Then, says Jesus, another 25% of the seed fall on stony ground, where there is very little earth. They grow up quickly, but because there is not enough soil, the sun scorches them up, and the plants do not survive, as they have inadequate roots. So on the streets of our area something suddenly catches on – but there is no foundation or background of stability, education, expectation or support. So the tender plant of new life is scorched. And since it has no root, it dies. Yet it was marvellous when it was alive – a new light in clouded eyes, a flash of brilliance in a broken life, a spark of wholeness in a chaos of fragments. And we have to be there for those things even if they are quickly scorched and wither away.

Other seeds fell among thorn bushes,
But as the thorns grew up,
They choked them,
And no grain came (v. 7).

Again, says Jesus, another 25% of the seed fall among thorns. The thorns grow alongside the corn, but in the end they are stronger than the corn and they choke it, so that the corn gets no more sun, and the grain never appears. So in our mission, our little projects, organizations and groups are constantly in danger of being swamped, or out-bid for money, or smothered by some larger initiative, or are simply unable to survive because of paucity of workers, resources or finance. But that does not mean that we should not be there, because we might not win. It means we should be there, even if we might fail. And it was not all failure, for along the way, we did something, we created something, we stood by something, we stood for something, which had its own glorious moment, which had authenticity and autonomy and holiness. Maybe the contemporary form of 'sin boldly' is 'fail gladly' – work at God's project, but don't be surprised if it fails. The biblical God, after all, had many projects that failed. So, with God, fail gladly.

Projects should be done

Other seeds fell into good soil,
They sprouted and grew,
And brought forth grain
Thirty fold, sixty fold and a hundred fold (v. 8).

Sometimes, though, Jesus concludes, you hit the jackpot. The final 25% of your seed get into good soil, where they mature and grow and bring forth an enormous return. Actually, a subsistence peasant farmer could exist on a return of 10%, but this sower gets a 30%, 60% and 100% yield – truly bumper stalks of grain. We have seen on our streets and in our places things catch on, movements grow, individuals get new life, people become communities, unexpected folk become colleagues and co-workers, the victimized become managers, the disorganized become organizers, tiny projects become big programmes. So, if only one out of four of our seeds remains long enough to bring a harvest, it is not only enough, but it is more than enough! So it is with our work. And so our work takes its place within the development of human kin-ship and human survival and human flourishing within the city.

We have seeds in the city, then. And we have a variety of soils, most of them problematic. And we have sowers, trying to get some good fruit out of often stony ground. The three factors are the subjects of this book – the soil, the seed and the sowers.

Look at the soil, first. Our soil is the ground in which we work, and into which we try to sow our seeds. The soil is the contemporary city and all the problems, tensions and issues which make up contemporary urban life. In this sense, this book is a more personal and human-level account of the realities which are summarized in the 1997 Methodist Report, *The Cities*.[1] I highlight here, from the point of view of some specific people and communities, some of the factors and questions dealt with in that Report. In particular, I concentrate on some of the specific characteristics and elements which seem so constant and endemic in the life of cities, not only in Britain but almost everywhere in modern conurbations across the globe. These characteristics and elements provide the context for our sowing and growing. Hopefully our work in our inner city ground might suggest ways of tackling some of the problems, which are relevant also for national and local government, as they seek partnerships to help improve the situation.

What is the seed we are trying to sow? To me, the seed is at least in part the search for some radical and relevant stories and models which might work for people getting their existence together in the modern world. My focus here is the individual or small group that wants to do something significant with their life in the context of the divided city. So, I share some of the motives and thinking of fellow disciples, locals and incomers, who look for clues in Christianity, and especially in the Gospels, for what they might do, and who experiment with lifestyles and practices which to them make sense in the light of the Gospel stories. This seed involves a Gospel-based discipleship spirituality which has come to be the basis of my own life, giving the sense that our stories are very like Gospel ones. I develop here the ground mapped out in *Radical Jesus* in 1986, but concentrate on individual Gospel stories.[2]

The sowers are the contemporary community builders in the cities, especially but not exclusively Christian ones. What actually can be done? More specifically, what can be done by small communities of committed people, at the base of our society? In this, I use my experience of thirty years' work in inner city Sheffield, and tell some of the stories of those unique and significant people and churches who constitute the Sheffield Inner City Ecumenical Mission – hereafter often simply SICEM. This book is offered as a celebration of a pilgrimage together, as well as an offering to others elsewhere of things we have discovered. I tried this first in *Into the City* in 1982.[3] This volume picks up the story again.

The three chapters which immediately follow deal specifically with these elements. Chapter 2 on People and Problems is about our 'soil', and provides a summary of some of the major characteristics of our area alongside an assessment of the larger urban issues of the country. The third chapter is called Seekers and Stories, the 'seeds' of our story, and picks up the wider issues of the contemporary search for meaningful life, with the inner city a crucible and a fulcrum. The fourth chapter, Communities and Churches, describes in outline the 'sowers', the congregations and people of our Mission, so that the reader may have a picture of the particular church communities whose stories are told later. Chapters 2 and 4 focus on two aspects of our title – chapter 2 on 'Sheffield' and 'Inner City', chapter 4 on 'Ecumenical' and 'Mission'.

The fifth chapter, Palestine and Pitsmoor, leads into the main part of the book, and explains the method of setting alongside one another the three elements just indicated – the soil, represented in various aspects of the secular context; the seed represented in the response of some story of individual disciples living by pieces of the Gospel; and the sowing, the response of some part of the local SICEM communities.

The chapters which follow all more or less begin with some story or experience of specific facets of the life in the inner city and its people. They then go on to indicate how disciples here see the relevance of some parts of Jesus' own life and ministry for their life and ministry. They finally describe aspects of our work which derive from our sense of call and commitment as people of the city and people of faith.

At the end, I return to the three areas in turn, and ask what is to be said on the basis of what we have experienced and discovered. I address some questions to the city, about what we need for our cities to flourish, in terms of new alliances and policies. I seek to engage fellow Christians, about what discipleship is needed today, and, indeed, about what discipleship actually is. Finally, I speak to the churches about the congregations, the ministries, and the mission we need for the future.

It is perhaps worth saying that I take the fact of 'seeds' in the city as a significant and even decisive factor. I believe that the hope for a better city in the future rests in the constant and repeated mystery and reality of seeds of change falling into the ground. So this is not just another book about how we can re-organize urban areas. It is, I trust, both thrilling and realistic about how we can all participate in a dynamic process of renewal and regeneration – how we can all be seeds of hope in the city.

# 2

# People and Problems

The stories in this book come out of a particular place, where particular people have lived and continue to live their lives. One of the best ways of encouraging each other, in the churches as anywhere else, is to swap stories. Left to ourselves, we tell each other stories. 'So, what's going on in your place?' 'Oh, I must tell you what's just happened to us.'

Behind every story there is an event, a happening, and a situation in which it originated. The rest of this book is about events. This chapter describes the context in which the happenings took place. In a dossier produced in 1997, we described our situation thus:

### Where We Are and Who We Are

We are in *Sheffield* – England's fourth largest city, a city set between Yorkshire plains and Derbyshire hills, a city of rich cultural life, a steel city, a city of industry, commerce and communications, with two universities, a new airport and rail links nationwide.

We are in the *Inner City* – in the north and north-east of the city's inner belt, in a variety of very varied communities, some multi-racial, with some living in council housing estates, some mixed Edwardian houses. We have many different races, cultures and religions, including a majority still of white working class and poor people. Sheffield's first and seventh worst 'Areas of Poverty' are in our areas.

Sheffield arouses a mixture of feelings. Nowadays, we are no longer the city of the failed World Student Games of 1992, nor yet the city of the so-far disastrous supertram of 1995, nor even of the longest serving Labour City Council, since this year, 1999, we turned Liberal Democrat, and await the future with some interest. We might still be the city of Meadowhall – for a time the largest shopping centre in Britain. But above all, since 1997, we are the city of *The Full Monty*, the film about six unemployed steel workers and their search for something worthwhile to do – in fact, to form a male strippers group.

*The Full Monty* has earned more than any other British film ever. All visitors to Sheffield have either seen it or find a way to see it when they arrive. Sheffield is now *The Full Monty* city, famed world-wide. Buses bring visitors on 'The Full Monty Tour' into our area, to visit the Shirecliffe helicopter pad where the lads exercised, or to the streets where they walked, or the Shiregreen Working Men's Club where the men's striptease show finally took place.

*The Full Monty* communicates effectively because it conveys in an archetypal way many of the realities of contemporary post-industrial cities which I will be describing. The film creates a world-wide sympathy because it is about the realities of people living in unemployment and in various degrees of poverty, who yet try to do something, against all the odds. I saw the film twice in New York, and it was clearly these elements which communicated and created empathy far away from our city.

The publicity 'commercial' of Sheffield in the 1960s which the film runs behind the initial titles is the Sheffield which many remember, with 90,000 people employed in the steel and related industries, and a stable city life based on those industries. It is the Sheffield I can just remember, as my family and I were sent to Sheffield in September 1970. We arrived in the inner city, a dilapidated and declining scene, with the first waves of post-war immigrants on the streets, more Afro-Caribbean then than Pakistani or Bengali. The first two chapters of *Into the City*[1] describe the situation we found, and some of its later chapters describe the Pitsmoor Action Group and the *Pitsmoor News* to which David Blunkett refers in his

Foreword. Nearly thirty years later, much has changed. By 1999, less than 10,000 are employed in steel or related industries, though interestingly, the output of steel has actually increased, using modern methods.

In 1993, the City Directorate of Planning and Economic Development published a Review of the City's Areas of Poverty called *Poverty and the Poor in Sheffield*.[2] The Report used the 1991 Census results plus Housing Benefit, Unemployment and Health statistics. Some of its basic comparative statistics have been updated in the 1999 *Benefits and Poverty in Sheffield*, a Review of the 1998 Housing Benefits Data, and in the 1999 Burngreave and Brightside Area Profiles.[3]

The Government's Social Exclusion Unit Report of 1998, *Bringing Britain Together*[4] highlights the gross inequalities across Sheffield. The Burngreave situation in 1999 highlights the comparisons between our side of the city and the more prosperous, western side. 39% of households in Burngreave are on Income Support, compared to 4% in Ecclesall. Unemployed people in Ecclesall are four times more likely to get a job than those in Burngreave. Unemployment in Burngreave is 22%, and over a third have been jobless for over a year. By Polling Districts, the December 1998 percentages of households on Housing Benefit, Community Tax and Income Support for areas covered by SICEM was Lopham 66.4%, Ellesmere 65.1%, Hinde House 52.3%, Pye Bank 50.4%, Valentine 47.1%, Concord 44.8%, Shiregreen 38.5%, Abbeyfield 38.1%, Whiteways 37.4%. Between 39% and 52% of dependent children grow up in households with no wage earner.

The Pye Bank District is one of our areas. It contains a mixture of two-storey houses, maisonettes and high rise flats built during the 1960s. In the 1980s, the Council housing stock was substantially refurbished through Estate Action. Over 85% of households are in Council accommodation and 81% of dwellings are flats, with 19% houses. The 1993 Report stated:

Pye Bank contains the most deprived communities in Sheffield:

61% in receipt of income support;
41% unemployed;
46% single parent families;
82% of all families with children have no wage earners;
84% of households have no access to a car.

Even the significant improvement of the council housing cannot alter the multiple deprivation suffered by the 2,523 people who live in this acute Area of Poverty. It is probable that even the 24% of the potential workforce which are in employment are largely in low paid, predominantly service sector employment.[5]

The 1993 Report stated that in the Nottingham Street, Firvale and Abbeyfield neighbourhoods, Afro-Caribbean and Asian people have a 'high level of unemployment, economic inactivity and long-term sickness', and 44.4% of all single parent families are Black. People with bad health, high death rates and drug use likewise concentrate in these areas.[6]

Pye Bank/Woodside is where The Furnival and the Ashram Houses are located, and is near to Pitsmoor Methodist Church, so we know the area pretty well. The various characteristics in the Pye Bank/Woodside description are typical of contemporary areas of deprivation in Britain. They amount to what many writers call 'multiple deprivation'. The various factors each build on the other to form a 'cycle of deprivation'.

· Poverty
˙ Unemployment    Homelessness
, Low pay            · Powerlessness
· Segregation             .Stigmatization
· Poor services          ˙ Drugs and crime
· Poor housing              ˙ Vandalism
˴ Poor health              · Delinquency
Different taces        ˴One parent families
· Isolation          Dereliction
Poor schools

The cycle of deprivation means that local people are more or less trapped by the situation and its problems. If they try to improve things at any one point, they are still held back by other points. Intervention at any one point will create some improvement, and will have some knock-on effect on some of the other points. But it will still be a hard struggle, and any of the other points of deprivation can continue or reappear. Thus, someone who breaks free of drugs and crime is still surrounded by the stigma of the area, the vandalism, the delinquency, the powerlessness, and the low pay and poverty, any or all of which too often keep them in acute deprivation even if they kick the habit.

The stories I shall tell will focus on various aspects of the cycle of deprivation, one by one. They will indicate how personally depressing and tragic they are. But they will also indicate how, in practice, on the streets, people can yet act significantly and courageously. This is not a facile suggestion about how everything can suddenly be improved. It is perhaps something more significant – a few cameos of how specific people actually do something in the face of specific problems.

It is also to insist that the focus should move away from the 'problems' of the inner cities to the people of the inner cities. The people are both the problem bearers and the problem victims. All the people do not have the same problems. It is the proximity of whole groups of people with various kinds of disadvantage which is the situation in these areas. But a decisively new feel is given to it all when the issues are seen in human terms. The cycle of deprivation becomes a circle of individuals, families and groups; each with their own problem, but multiplying their disadvantages by being together in the same places. Many of the people have more than one of the problems themselves, but they are surrounded by others, each of whom also belongs to more than one of the need groups.

So look at the cycle of deprivation as a circle of deprived people:

Poor people

Jobless people    Homeless people

Low paid workers    Powerless people

Segregated people    Stigmatized people

Neglected people    Drug addicts and criminals

People in bad housing    Vandals

Sick folk    Delinquents

Immigrants    Single mums & dads

Isolated folk    People in derelict areas

Poorly educated folk

So, in the chapters which follow, the stories of some of the 'problems' are told in terms of specific individuals, families and groups, the people.

However, some readers might think, is this really the full picture of contemporary Sheffield? Are there not success stories as well? Of course, there are, and they need to be added for a total picture. But there are two sides to that argument. I recall David Hobson, the chair of the Sheffield Chamber of Commerce Regeneration Committee, writing an article on 'Look to City Centres', urging 'a more strategic approach to town centres, particularly areas of transport, funding for regeneration, planning, and to encourage a more welcoming city centre'.

I sent a reply called 'Looking to a "Whole City"', which the *Sheffield Telegraph* published as its Opinion column the next week (25 April 1997). I agreed with David Hobson's main point, and added two further ones:

First, we need to start looking at our city as a whole, and not as competing segments. At the end of the day, Meadowhall will suffer if only Meadowhall exists! And the city centre will suffer if there is not a totally renewed transport system in the whole city. In the complex interrelations of the modern city, we all succeed together or we all hang together. Now that steel affects fewer of us, and the sports face of Sheffield still quavers, we need to know what Sheffield is. There are too many competing bits and pieces, unrelated, and too many failed segments. Will someone start putting it all together?

I referred to *The Cities Report*, which made a similar point, stressing that 'new mechanisms must be developed by Central Government, to assess the full social, economic and environmental costs and benefits of proposed public policy interventions in Britain's cities'.[7] I went on in the article:

> The second priority is that we need to produce a more inclusive city. While the Attercliffe/Don Valley and the city centre squabble for resources, we need also to look at the effects of either on the run down areas surrounding them. I live in Pitsmoor, and it has been galling over the years to see the disappearance of worthwhile jobs for local men (mainly), only to be replaced by part-time, often under-paid work by women (mainly) 'servicing' offices and shops down the valley. A major need is to extend the wealth of city centre and valley developments so that local people benefit. As our Report says: 'Government funded programmes to help relieve unemployment in city districts should concentrate on: reconnecting unemployed city dwellers with recruitment channels and labour markets, especially young and long-term unemployed people; developing application skills and self esteem; and radically improving the quality of vocational education and training.'[8]

The reality is that the city centre and Meadowhall will not survive in a situation in which increasing numbers are excluded, creating a divided society, with no-go areas and large groups of people not participating in the city's life. I agree, then, that we do not want to keep the divided city going forever. But we need new policies actually to change it – then we'll have different stories to tell.

The European Commission's current Nomenclature of Territorial Units for Statistics (NUTS) indicated that Gross National Product (GNP) for South Yorkshire sub-region in 1997 was only £7,797 – below the then Objective 1 regions of Merseyside (£7.874). Highlands and Islands (£8,484) and Northern Ireland (£8,535).[9] So that South Yorkshire from 1999 is Britain's No. 1

Region of Poverty. Consequently, from January 2000, South Yorkshire is receiving Objective 1 Funding from the European Community. Currently, community groups and the voluntary sector, including elements of SICEM, are involved in planning bits of the new enterprise.

# 3

# Seekers and Stories

'Seekers' in the contemporary world come in all shapes and sizes.

There are the young people who, surrounded by all the demands for upward mobility and success, yet still look elsewhere for inspiration and happiness. There are the people in their thirties and forties, who have tried a business or professional life, and suddenly feel that they want to do something different. There are the people in mid-life, whose 'mid-life crisis' makes them question the domestic or career arrangements they have so carefully built around themselves, and ask 'Is there life before death?' There are the people around sixty, with a third of their life still ahead of them, who want to know what else there is to do, besides caring for the garden, and cleaning empty bedrooms.

Seekers – I meet them still in universities, in conferences, in suburban churches, in voluntary organizations.

Now, I know that there are many armchair seekers. They are engaged in a safe journey of mind and spirit, which never runs the risk of error or tragedy, because it never moves them from where they are. And there are also many butterfly seekers. They flit from this interest to that, taking their world with them, never affecting people or realities in the real world, endlessly doing things 'for the experience'.

But there are also serious seekers. They are perhaps overcome by the realities of poverty, or of disadvantage, or of injustice, or just of things as they are. They perhaps know or experience some of the factors of deprivation summarized in the last chapter. We encourage visitors to come to our area and see for

themselves, in weekend courses, or inner city retreats or place-
ments. Sometimes they can be really changing experiences.

Some who come are not Christians, but are just curious as to
whether there are any alternative life patterns worth pursuing,
and any alternative places to be.

So, hopefully, a few 'seekers' will read these pages. They will
find some very 'alternative' stories. They are the stories of communities of people and of individuals, people whose lives are, in
contemporary political, social and cultural terms, more or less
insignificant. They are not the stories of great people, or of great
events. They do not take place in any notable context. They
are often passed by without being noticed in the media. Or if
some particular story catches the headlines, the total story does
not.

They are stories of significance partly because of the conviction of the actors and communities involved, that somehow
their stories relate to the dramatic and unprecedented view of
life and all things represented by a certain character in history
called Jesus. And among the followers of this Jesus all down
through history, there has always been a kind of game or
competition going on. Who has got bits of their existence or
experience or practice which cohere with, or belong to the same
reality as, or could be said to be part of the same story as, the
fundamental and originating mystery known by the name of
Jesus? Or even, who has got more striking bits than others, in
their context or in their time?

My hope is that it might help others to discern how the Jesus
impetus works, if we hear the way it works in one particular
group of people – the group of people in the Sheffield inner city,
who work together in the branches of the ecumenical mission.
In this chapter, I want to try to explain this hope, and to do so
by describing how this book has come out the way it has.

In *Stirrings: Essays Christian and Radical*, the volume of
essays which I edited in 1976, Bishop John D. Davies wrote of
how theology waits for people re-writing parts of the Jesus
story with their own lives, just as the New Testament is the
witness to the actions of the first followers.

The most urgent mandate to the church is surely to enable God's story to continue to happen in the world. The New Testament is the story and the evidence of the effect of Christ on people, not only through the activities of Jesus of Nazareth but through the community of faith which derived from his activities. This is how faith was transformed into story; later, men came along with their words and pens and put the story into the form in which we have received it. But the writing always comes after the happening.

One day, someone may be able to write down the story of how faith happened amid the disorders and despairs of our contemporary society, But, before the story can be told it must be acted: and that is the activity of faith. Our task is to get on with making the story.[1]

Some of us have had a go at it, and we can perhaps now venture to tell some of the stories. Indeed, this is my third attempt at it! The stories develop – and move on – and so, too does one's perception of what is happening.

First, in 1982, in *Into the City*, I found myself interpreting the first twelve years of SICEM in terms of the elements and dynamics in the pattern of Jesus' ministry and mission. It seemed that there was a theological sequence in the ministry of Jesus. So the stories of my own coming into Sheffield in 1970, and my own attempts to learn what it meant to be in ministry here, were illuminated by some leading stages or categories in Jesus' ministry as described in the Gospels. It began with 'Incarnation', arriving and digging in, and immediately became 'being used' by people in need – 'Healing'. It moved on to looking around for messages already there – 'Parables', and trying out a few token first attempts at action – 'Acted Parables'. More and more it involved working with very small communities – 'Disciple Groups'. And as we got into Jesus-style action, we found ourselves facing 'Crucifixion', which proved in practice the door to 'Resurrection', and to glimpses of a 'New City' – a 'Parousia'. Thus, Incarnation – Healing – Parables – Acted Parables – Disciple Groups – Crucifixion – Resurrection –

Parousia became an eight-stage 'Gospel Pattern Dynamics' which we used in teaching and thinking.[2]

Then, in 1986, in *Radical Jesus*, I retold the story of Jesus in Mark's Gospel as a story understandable in our time as that of a local inner city community activist, who identified with the local people in need, declared that things could get better, and had a clear 'Project' – the revealing and the establishment of the Kingdom of God. He worked in solidarity with the poor, celebrated parties in the homes of the socially excluded, entered into partnership with women, and opened the door to foreigners. Jesus' ministry is that of a people's politician, a counter-politician, and a leader of a Journey Downwards, which celebrates alternative realities and anti-social norms, and who heads a mini-movement of protest and affirmation of a radically alternative culture – the Kingdom of God – which is defeated by the powers, and then re-asserted in resurrection.[3]

Fundamentally, I have tried to live my ministry in the inner city in the light of these two pictures of Jesus. The first teaches me that there are different modes, styles, times and tasks, elements in a sequence. The second teaches me that as a community minister, I already have a strong model and project in the person and work of the radical leader of a movement acting in the light of a Divine Project – the Kingdom of God. These two models give me a strong sense of movement and expectation.

But then, there are the events of every day life and every day ministry. How do they fit in? Well, I found myself basically believing that Jesus' ministry and work were 'like' those of a community minister in an area like ours. But the life of a community minister, I reflected, was all bits and pieces, all tiny fragments, insignificant actions, passing experiences, temporary relationships. It was a mixture of long disappointments and sudden successes, deep heartbreak and incredible faithfulness. It was people holding on in impossible situations, people being exposed to vicious oppressors, people being made aliens and enemies on their own streets. It was youngsters running away from life, mums trying to keep it all together, babies born without secure homes, parents thrown out by landlords, tenants deceived by take-overs far away in the city, authorities coming in from outside to lay down the law, marches of protest into the city.

Then it came to me. It was not only the grand sweep of Jesus' life from Incarnation to Parousia that was in my experience and in my bones and in my context. It was not only the movement and project for radical community change that was happening all around me. It was also the nitty-gritty, particular and unrepeatable happenings, and not less the dull slog and the long haul, that were replete with Gospel-story resonance, and pregnant with Gospel 'good news' and revelation and ultimacy. It was the Jesus of the streets. And the streets of Jesus were as full of the list of dramas and people and happenings and communities and enemies and heroes and heroines and betrayers and crucifiers – as were my streets.

The sequence of stages and motifs, and the story of the movement and the project, were mediated in the Gospels themselves by the succession of apparently artless and fortuitous happenings in which Jesus found himself involved. These were the occasions of his teaching, the backdrop for his Kingdom, the bread and butter of his movement and his community. Just as mine are for me! And his happenings on his streets turned out to be incredibly like our happenings on our streets!

So, I found myself picking my way through the singular happenings around Jesus that got recorded in the Gospels, with a new thrill and a new expectation. Which bits and which people, which scenes and which happenings, are coming alive around me now? How can I extend and deepen my perception of and commitment to the things around me in inner city Sheffield, through recognizing that the Master I seek to serve only fulfilled his ministry and vocation by picking his way among the bits and pieces of the places where he was? His 'Project' had to start and continue with the dull specificities of particular people, places, meetings, events, communities and political realities. If my life was similarly bound by the limitations of particular people, places, meetings, events, communities and political realities, then I was at least in the right place to begin to try to follow him.

Hence, in this book, everything is very small, and very specific. The stories sometimes have names, sometimes not. The tales are sometimes told in detail, sometimes just in headlines. In some cases, the particular minister or disciple in SICEM is named and quoted, in other cases not. If you look at the Gospels, of course, you will find that the stories about Jesus are also told in exactly this variety of ways. Sometimes, names are given, or full stories are told. At other times, only hints, slogans, and snapshots survive.

I began to teach myself and those with me to see themselves and their ministries in the light of the Gospel ministry of Jesus. And especially, to do this in the special way in which the Gospel ministry of Jesus comes down to us, notably in the form of very particular stories of very particular people in very particular situations. The Jesus stories are replete with all the bits of 'occasion' and 'particularity' and 'oddity' that our stories are today. So that it might even be some element in the occasion or particularity or oddity of our story that gets us into some part of the Jesus stories.

The trick became to ask, 'When have I seen this Gospel story on our streets or in our community or in some individual?' 'When has this odd bit of Gospel happening taken place again in our midst?' 'Which of the Gospel elements is alive and well in our particular place?'

The tradition calls this 'Work on the Word'. It goes on in SICEM in a variety of ways. The preachers, lay and ordained, as they go round the churches Sunday by Sunday, frequently tell the stories of current happenings in the churches and in the local communities, and this often means using particular Gospel happenings to elucidate or expand what has been taking place. Happily, our preachers do not have to follow any pre-scribed lectionary. They are free to follow the 'reading' or lectionary of the community or of the disciples or of the street, and expect and look for Gospel and Epistle which are provoked by and thus expand and theologize upon, the Gospel happenings all around us. So, a happening in the community, or in the life of the churches, or in someone's experience, gets lifted up in the light of the Gospel, and its story gets taken round the churches, often outside SICEM as well.

Sometimes there are intentional and planned times of reflection, either within the small group of church or project members involved in an action or piece of community work, or else when a whole church, branch or unit meets specifically for theological reflection. Every now and then, SICEM as a whole meets for a half day of sharing and reflection. And stories are shared in the SICEM Community Work Committee and the Preachers' Meeting. Each May, the Preachers' Meeting arranges a series of evening Bible studies taken by them. For fifteen years, I took an annual sermon on 'The State of the Mission' around the churches, each time reflecting on a Gospel passage or theme which seemed present in our life together. The Annual Report of the Mission has also observed scriptural antecedents, as when in two consecutive years we reflected on the Gospel perspectives of journey backwards, journey sideways and journey downwards, visible in aspects of the mission's life.

Sometimes the 'word' is an insight into a piece of the Gospel drama, and a compelling sense of 'call' which derives from it, which has come to an individual. Hence, some of the chapters here carry the names of individual people or ministers who have perceived a link between a Gospel reality and a present possibility, and have begun to plan or create a project as a present 'recapitulation' of the Gospel dynamic.

All Christians, of course, are invited to play out such 'imaginative identification'[4] on their own experiences, in their own contexts. Other disciples might feel, at the end, that despite all the problems, inner city disciples have the good fortune to be in situations remarkably like those of the Gospels, because they have a privileged position from which to view their practice, and the practice recorded in the Gospels.[5] In UTU's Urban Ministry Courses, we do this kind of analysis of situations in some detail. Each participant does a 'situation analysis' of their own area, community, neighbourhood, church and base group.[6] We then invite them to do a situation analysis of a Gospel or other biblical book, and see what learnings follow.

There is another implication of my 'discoveries' of Jesus' pattern beginning with Incarnation, of his ministry as community activist and prophet, and of his total engagement with and growth through particular incidents and people. It is that we primarily involve ourselves in Christian existence, and we are primarily involved by the Spirit in the life of Christ, through action, through practice, through discipleship.[7] The question then is, how can I discover Jesus-coherent or theologically coherent action, practice, discipleship? Imaginative identification with Gospel actions is one way of doing this. It is not so much the frequently urged 'theological reflection on action'. It is much more 'theological practice', which I enter into, or find myself in, which I then reflect on. The theology is in the practice, not primarily in the reflection after it. So as a seeker, the stories are my own way into reflecting the practice of Jesus in parts of my practice. Such, at any rate, is the matter of this book.

# 4

# Communities and Churches

The Sheffield Inner City Ecumenical Mission was formed in 1971. It is essentially an alliance of small congregations and small communities, deeply committed to their own neighbourhoods, distinctive styles and ethos, who seek to support each other. SICEM constitutes an 'umbrella', under which the churches' own existence and mission can be secured and enhanced, and under which they can work with each other in practical ways when this is felt necessary or appropriate.[1]

The Foundation and Constitution document of 1971 begins with five 'Foundation Principles', the first of which is 'The will to share mission, ministries, planning, personnel, plant, resources, in the belief that the Common Life of the whole church as the body of Christ must be manifest in the world'. Everything else follows from this. The Foundation Principles go on to speak of 'a common faith', of 'varying styles, emphases and forms of worship', and 'variety of experiment', 'the mutual recognition of different emphases in belief, within a common trust and acceptance'. Individual congregations and units 'retain their present individuality and distinctive character, and this is seen as an advance towards true catholicity'. Ecclesiastically, SICEM is an 'Area of Ecumenical Partnership', and has its own Sponsoring Committee to protect and advocate its distinctive ethos.[2]

Thus, the Mission works 'bottom upwards'.[3] The churches and units themselves are its core and *raison d'être*. They are located in the north and north-east inner city and outer estates of Sheffield, between the city centre and the M1 motorway. We are on the north side of the Don valley, formerly the steel works valley, now the site of the Sheffield Development Corporation buildings, the Sports Stadiums and the Meadowhall shopping complexes. Our branches' locations can be gathered from the diagram of SICEM Branches (p. 28). The diagram illustrates a fundamental principle of SICEM – that we are 'both traditional and experimental'. We have three fairly traditional style 'church' buildings, though each is multi-purpose – St James, Shiregreen and Wincobank. We have one modern church building, part of a housing complex – Pitsmoor. We have three branches based in shops – Grimesthorpe, New Roots/Ashram, and the Burngreave Ashram. We have two branches based in houses – Urban Theology Unit and Ashram Houses. We have one branch based in a former pub – The Furnival. This variety of locations is important to us, and mirrors the diversity of our area, and the diversity we ourselves feel is the appropriate form for Mission in our time.

We have always understood 'ecumenical' to mean involving different churches in shared mission. Our branches do not have to be 'united' churches. As our Foundation Principles state, our aim is 'sharing of mission, ministries, planning, personnel, plant and resources', not amalgamation of denominational congregations. Thus, two Methodist and two URC churches remain denominational, though their memberships are increasingly multi-denominational.

However, Ashram Community Trust was ecumenical since its foundation in 1967 – only its Sheffield branches are a branch of SICEM. UTU was ecumenical by its Constitution in 1969 – denominations were not mentioned! The Upper Wincobank Schools Trust was set up in 1880 on the basis that it was for charitable purposes, and 'If such purposes include the use of the premises as a place of worship, it shall be for the simple preaching of Christ's Gospel, without any exclusive or sectarian or denominational bias.'

When The Furnival developed in 1996, the building remained Methodist, but the congregation quickly became multi-denominational. Methodist, URC and Baptist authorities, plus Churches Together in South Yorkshire, led us through nine

# SICEM BRANCHES

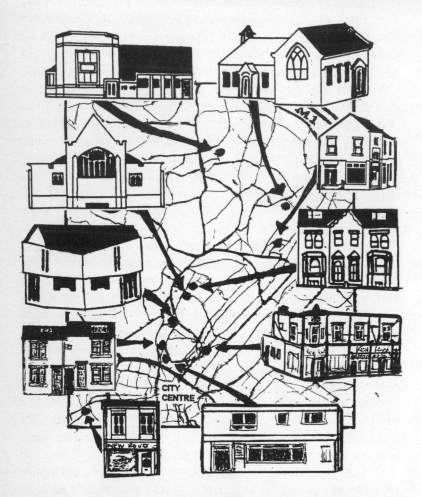

Clockwise from top left: Shiregreen United Reformed Church, Upper Wincobank Undenominational Chapel, Grimesthorpe Methodist Shop Church, Urban Theology Unit, Burngreave Ashram Shop & Centre, The Furnival, Rock Street Ashram House, New Roots Ashram Centre, Pitsmoor Methodist Church and Centre, St James United Reformed Church drafts of a Constitution before the final one in January 1998. The Constitution names the three denominations, and also the Anglican and Roman Catholic churches, as members of those churches are also in the Furnival congregation. And, even more significant, there are people from no previous church who have joined. We tried to get the word 'post-denominational' into the Constitution, but that proved too much for the denominations!

But we really are Christian communities which are no longer denominational or even inter-denominational. More and more, our understanding of 'ecumenical' is broadening. Anglicans and RCs have always been members of UTU and Ashram, alongside many other denominations. And more and more, the life of our branches is becoming 'post-denominational'. A count of the thirteen members in Grimesthorpe in 1999 revealed previous denominational allegiances as five Methodist, three Anglican, three Baptist, one Unitarian, one Church of Scotland. Denominations are not relevant on our streets, and the differences we celebrate between our branches are less and less along denominational lines.

As the individual churches and units are the background and the *dramatis personae* of our book, it will be useful to describe them in turn now, so that the reader can check back on the scenes and situations of the later chapters. The founding units in 1971 were Andover Street, Burngreave Road and Lopham Street Methodist Churches and St James Presbyterian Church, followed in 1972 by Grimesthorpe Methodist and Ashram House, and then by UTU (1973), Shiregreen URC (1978) and Upper Wincobank (1980). I describe them in this historical order.

St James United Reformed Church, originally Presbyterian, dates from 1910. In 1995, it had a major internal face-lift and remodelling, financed by the building of twelve single persons' housing flats on part of the site. St James is on the corner of two roads of Edwardian semi-detached houses, now a multi-racial area, with UTU's back entrance over the other side of Scott Road. UTU students are catered for in St James' weekly lunch club run till recently by its elderly members. Meetings and organizations cater for various local groups. St James has been a striking example of a church with significant Afro-Caribbean membership, since they were first welcomed in the 1960s.

Andover Street and Burngreave Road churches united in 1973 to form the Pitsmoor Methodist Church. A new building was opened in 1975, an Upper Room Church and a lower level Community Centre, built as a part of the Foundry Housing Association complex of thirty-one housing units. It is on the main Burngreave Road, in the middle of the cosmopolitan, multi-racial inner city. It has a major commitment in old people's lunch clubs and in the Monday Special Needs Club. Pitsmoor has our largest community rooms, useful for many purposes.

The Furnival is a Local Ecumenical Partnership, opened in September 1996. Its four founding members had been at Lopham Street Methodist Church until it was sold in March 1996. The Furnival is on the Pye Bank/Woodside Estate, Sheffield's most deprived area, within the Burngreave Ward. The Furnival now has offices on the first floor, a youth education project in the cellar, an open café in the main bar, and an activities room/quiet room/worship centre in the lounge bar

Grimesthorpe Methodist Church occupies two shops on the corner of Wansfell Road and Birdwell Road. The area is a 1900s urban village of terraced houses, built for steelworkers, the old steel works valley of Attercliffe being nearby. The area now has a mix of older residents and young families plus families of Pakistani origin. Over the shops is a flat for two or three residents. Old People's Lunch Club and Children's Club bring neighbours into what has become a very participatory neighbourhood community centre.

Ashram Community Trust is a small nationwide charity (No. 290459) formed in 1967. Its Sheffield branch is a SICEM member, and currently has houses and projects – the New Roots shop, Ashram centre and flat at 347 Glossop Road, opposite the university; the two Ashram community houses presently at 75 and 77 Rock Street; the new Burngreave Ashram on Spital Hill; and the midweek 'Upper Room', an evening communal meal, worship and meeting at 178 Abbeyfield Road, continuing the life of the former Eucharist Congregation (1974–97), itself a SICEM branch.

Urban Theology Unit is a registered charity (No. 505334), formed in 1969 as an independent ecumenical urban theological and missional training agency, a 'community of study and action'. People of all ages, churches and interests come from all over the country – and overseas – to share their lives and explore new ways of ministry, vocation, theology and service. It is housed in four Edwardian semi-detached residences, 206–208–210–212 Abbeyfield Road, a street-level 'campus' with offices, libraries, resource rooms and kitchens, together with bedsits and flats for visiting students.

Shiregreen United Reformed Church was built as a Congregational Church in 1933, as a worship and community centre in the middle of the Shiregreen housing estate, reckoned as one of the largest 1930s estates in the country. The community hall now houses a parents and children project, and three old people's lunch clubs cater for thirty to forty old people each. The recent Project Report 1997 indicates a wide variety of community involvement, and much joint work with city-wide projects.

Upper Wincobank Undenominational Chapel was opened in 1840 as a village school, and then as a chapel in 1880. The Flower Estate, which now surrounds it, was one of the earliest 'Garden Villages', built in 1904. The estate was extended in the 1920s, and largely rebuilt in the 1980s, but has a reputation for being a city 'dumping ground'. In 1999, yet another demolition and rebuilding scheme is under way. The old schoolmaster's house is now a community house, in which individuals and families have come to live and share in the work in the chapel and neighbourhood.

SICEM internal organization and mutual support is provided by the SICEM Council, the SICEM Preachers' Meeting, the SICEM Team Ministry, and the SICEM Community Work Committee. There is also a major commitment to Pitsmoor and Shiregreen Community Transport, which runs two minibuses which service the ten SICEM old people's lunch clubs and other activities.

SICEM's relations with the denominations are handled by the SICEM Sponsoring Committee, which has three Methodist, three URC and two Baptist representatives, plus one each from the SICEM member branches which are themselves ecumenical, notably UTU, Ashram Community and the Undenominational Chapel. In addition, the Team Ministry and Chair of SICEM Council, plus representatives of the Anglican and Roman Catholic Churches, Churches Together in South Yorkshire and Sheffield Council of Churches are present as non-voting observers. The responsibilities and relationships both internal and external are indicated in the diagram of SICEM Relationships (p. 33). The Furnival Sponsoring Committee has the same membership as the SICEM Sponsoring Committee, as all the wider participating denominations of The Furnival are already there.

Ministry in SICEM has been consistently seen as the ministry of all its members. When in 1995 the Mission Council invited all member units to comment on their view of ministry, and their future ministry needs, the ministry of all unit members was the first priority. Indeed, for four and a half years, from 1985 to 1989, eight Local Pastors carried on the basic ministerial tasks, I myself being the only ordained minister. Leadership in SICEM rested heavily on long-term members like Amy Richinson, Barbara Swift, Mary Presswood and Barry Swift, while leadership in the churches was exercised by the Local Pastors – principally Mary Presswood at Pitsmoor (Pam Eaton from 1991), John Tomlinson at Shiregreen, Anne Digby at Lopham Street, Grace Vincent at Grimesthorpe, Glenys Ward at Wincobank. Each congregation made a detailed agreement with its Local Pastor as to responsibilities, length of service, and regarding any payments that were to be made – not everyone was paid.

As for ordained colleagues, Ian Lucraft (Methodist) was minister at Pitsmoor and Lopham Street from 1974 to 1985, and Victor Sheldrick and Faitala Talapusi (URC) ministered at

# SICEM RELATIONSHIPS

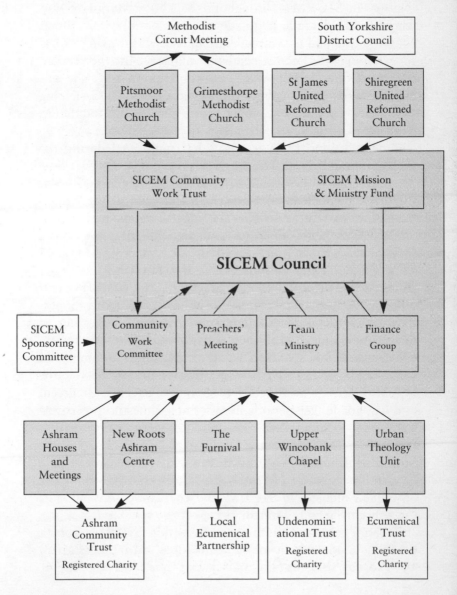

*Methodist Branches*  *United Reformed Branches*

Methodist Circuit Meeting

South Yorkshire District Council

Pitsmoor Methodist Church

Grimesthorpe Methodist Church

St James United Reformed Church

Shiregreen United Reformed Church

SICEM Community Work Trust

SICEM Mission & Ministry Fund

**SICEM Council**

SICEM Sponsoring Committee

Community Work Committee

Preachers' Meeting

Team Ministry

Finance Group

Ashram Houses and Meetings

New Roots Ashram Centre

The Furnival

Upper Wincobank Chapel

Urban Theology Unit

Ashram Community Trust

Registered Charity

Local Ecumenical Partnership

Undenomin-ational Trust

Registered Charity

Ecumenical Trust

Registered Charity

*Ecumenical Branches*

St James and Shiregreen in this period. Duncan Wilson (URC) was minister at St James, Shiregreen, Pitsmoor and Lopham Street from 1989 to 1997.[4] Ian and Duncan were the two long-serving colleagues and friends who shared in most of my ministry in SICEM. Throughout the 1980s Marjory Swift, who was an elder in St James, developed a ministry role in that congregation, and as a direct consequence was drawn to offer for training for non-stipendiary ministry in the United Reformed Church. Following her ordination in 1992 she was appointed to a new ministry support role in the URC, helping to initiate community contacts in churches in the South Yorkshire District, until her tragically early death in 1995.

Ordained ministry in SICEM has multiplied during the present decade, largely through UTU's policy of part-time appointments with local church pastorates. Inderjit Bhogal (Methodist) has been from 1994 part-time minister at Wincobank, but mainly at Urban Theology Unit, as Director of Studies from 1994 to 1997 and as Director from 1997. Jane Grinonneau (Baptist) has been minister at The Furnival since 1996, initally also part-time at UTU. Christine Jones (Methodist) arrived in 1997 as Director of Studies at UTU, and part-time minister at Grimesthorpe and Methodist Superintendent. Janet Lees (URC) arrived in 1998 as minister at Pitsmoor, St James and Shiregreen, without UTU responsibility.

During the twenty-seven years of my full-time ministerial work in SICEM, I have been minister or Interim Moderator for short periods at all SICEM branches except Shiregreen, and was for longer periods minister at Grimesthorpe (1972–97), Wincobank (1980–94) and Eucharist Congregation (1974–97), as well as being Director of UTU and Methodist Superintendent (1970–97). Since 1997, I have been a part-time core staff member and lecturer at UTU, and have continued as an unpaid minister in SICEM and chaplain/co-ordinator of the Ashram Sheffield Branch.

Urban Theology Unit has grown within SICEM from a part-time student body of six with three spare-time staff in 1973 to 103 students (still mainly part-time) and three full or majority time and twenty-one part-time staff in 1999. UTU's story will be told in a forthcoming volume, *Theology From the City*. Of Roy Crowder and Ed Kessler, colleagues from 1973, Roy left in 1982, Ed stayed until 1996. Of the current core staff, Ian Duffield joined in 1985, Jan Royan in 1993, Robin Pagan in 1994. Margaret Mackley was Co-ordinator, 1981–94, with Peter Colby as Administrator 1994–2000, and Janet Colby from 2000 as Support Services Manager. Inderjit, Christine, Janet, Ian, Jan, Robin and myself are currently the core staff.

The stories of the SICEM branches and ministries up to 1982 are contained in an earlier volume, *Into the City*, and I have not repeated them here. The stories in the present volume obviously depend heavily on current friends and colleagues, who are named in the chapters – and who have checked what is here attributed to them!

# 5

# Palestine and Pitsmoor

The stories of the Bible are obviously attractive, fascinating, odd, arbitrary, controversial, biased, one-sided – and commend themselves to you, depending on who you are, and where you are, and what your commitments are.

From their origin, this is what is to be expected. The stories were written not so much as impartial historical records of things as they actually happened, but as tales of the unexpected which were designed to sustain particular groups of people in their commitments, lifestyles and special destinies – to make them feel, despite much evidence to the contrary, that there was still a God and that such a God was on their side; and, more particularly, that the God who did singular and unexpected things with certain singular and unexpected people in past times was still doing similar things with similar people in new times.

Even the most apparently transparent biblical tale is told for a purpose, with some specific intention, with certain end results in view in terms of actions, attitudes, beliefs and convictions on the part of the readers.

Consequently there are at least three large questions which people who want to use the Bible have to face.

First, there is a question about the stories and the events in them:

If these stories were told
of certain odd and controversial events,
taking place in dark, unnoticed and unexpected places,
long ago, on the streets of Galilee and Judea,

What odd and controversial events
taking place in dark, unnoticed and unexpected places,
today, on the streets of our cities,
might be felt to be
in the same world as the biblical ones,
and thus perhaps become also
new parts of the ongoing divine sagas?

So, the first question is about the things which actually took place, which were told in the stories, and told to other people to provoke in them an expectation and a preparedness that the happenings behind the stories might be their experience also. If we take a simple example, Jesus' declaration of his mission in Mark 1. 14–15 is a striking claim regarding the arrival of the Kingdom. What would that mean as a claim on our streets today?

The second question reminds us of the fact that a story is something written down as a way of one person telling something to another person. It is a question about the people who told these stories, and the people to whom and for whom they were told:

If certain people told these stories
to shore up attitudes, beliefs, ways of life and expectations
which were extraordinary and God inspired then,
in the old times,
What kind of
attitudes, beliefs, ways of life and expectations
of people today
might feel identified with the biblical ones
and thus might feel incorporated
in the divine mysteries contained there?

This second question is about the storytellers, the original writers and the people around them – fellow disciples, questioners, critics. And it is also about the first readers, the hearers of the stories, the audiences who re-contextualized the messages and lived from them in their own lives. So, we could ask of Mark 1. 14–15, both who was Jesus, and who were the storytellers and the later disciples? What might it be like to identify with them?

The third question lands us fair and square back in our own time, with ourselves, our families, our community, our livelihood, our Christian friends, our problems and our questions. It is the question that takes us out on to the streets again:

> If things like this happened
> that got into these stories
> as the acts of God,
> What happenings could we get up to
> which would constitute
> the acts of God today?

The most decisive question is the one about discovering coherent following, faithful action, God-grounded practice, in our own lives today. So we need to know for Mark 1. 14–15, what actually happened when the Kingdom appeared, from the stories in the Gospel? And what might we expect to be happening today?

In this book, I record how I ended up with these questions, from living and celebrating some of the decisive stories in the Gospels concerning Jesus of Nazareth.

It was not that I thought it all out first. It was that certain occasions, or the prospect of them, or stories about them, provoked in me the recollection of some of the occasions in the Gospel stories. So, I found myself being drawn into a growing and progressively self-revealing series of mysteries whereby the original biblical stories happened again, achieved a new mutation, as part of some ongoing incarnation in the midst of the streets where I work, and among the people with whom I share my discipleship journey.

So, I thought it would be a proper activity of my discipleship – and afterwards worth sharing – to play the Gospel stories over within the context of the place where I work – in my case the inner city. I would read the stories 'from the bottom', not from outside. I would stand beside the mysteries of the places and situations and people and happenings of an inner city mission, and see where and when and how the mysteries of the first Christian stories provoked feelings of commonness and familiarity, so that we found ourselves saying: 'We've been here before,' because the deeds and stories of Jesus had been here before – or are here again – and would be here again and again as disciples at all times and in every different place waited for the coming of the Lord on their own streets. I would expect, look for, and facilitate the re-incarnations of the primary incarnation in Galilee and Jerusalem in my own pieces of reality, in Pitsmoor and Sheffield.

The Bible study method which is used in these studies is that which I describe in more detail as the method of Snap-Studies-Spinoff. In *Mark at Work*,[1] John D. Davies and I work out ways in which we can 'get into' Bible stories, and allow them to 'get into us'. The three stages we suggest are:

1. 'Snap'  What story in my own life or community matches up with, or clicks with, snaps with, this biblical story?
2. 'Study'  What more can I learn about the situation and circumstances of the biblical story, to fill out my instinctive 'snap'?
3. 'Spinoff'  What do I discover once I have found my way into this biblical story about what it might lead to in my own life?

Each chapter of the present book thus includes at least one Gospel passage, includes a 'Snap' story from today, and indicates what arose as 'Spinoff' implications for discipleship in our local setting. There are also at times suggestions about what by implication might arise as 'spinoffs' for the readers in their situation.

Readers who are interested in contemporary studies of the Bible might be glad to know that the three approaches, and the method just outlined, have interesting parallels in scholarly writing today. Indeed, those interested in contemporary biblical studies will have possibly unexpected contributions to their studies from what follows.

The first question, about the actions behind the stories, has been with us for some time. It became explicit in the theology of 'the God who acts' in the post-war period of 'biblical theology'. More recently, a new line has emerged, whereby attention is drawn to the fact that you can trace down the ages the way that an action recorded in scripture has reappeared , or at least been quoted as authority for further actions. Ulrich Luz, of Switzerland, calls this 'The History of Events', or 'The History of Happenings', or 'The History of Outworkings'. The German word he uses is *Wirkungsgeschichte*.[2] In the chapters which follow, I will be indicating some of the 'outworkings' – either conscious or unconscious – of some of the stories of the Gospels in my context.

The second question was about the readers and the writers. So far as the writers are concerned, we have had over the last twenty to thirty years many theories as to their purposes, techniques, methods and inner intentions. We called the study 'Editorial Criticism' or 'Redaction Criticism' (*Redaktionsgeschichte*). In the last ten years, there has been increasing interest in the readers as well as the writers. 'Reader Response Criticism' and 'Audience Criticism' have been the result. Any contemporary book on Gospel studies would describe this.[3] Our 'audience' or 'hearers' or 'readers' in inner city Sheffield have in fact thus become a new phenomenon which is properly a factor in contemporary biblical studies. 'How are these stories being read or heard?' inevitably means 'What sense are particular disciples getting out of them?' And that opens wide the door within biblical studies for precisely the 'new hearings' recorded here.

The third question, about our discipleship 'spinoffs' today, is one that biblical scholars do not as yet quite know how to deal with. It is easier for them to think and write about ancient happenings and ancient writers and readers – and even contemporary modern readers. It is not so easy to write about contemporary users of the events and the stories. But it is a proper question: 'What are the contemporary disciple-acts which these primary acts and writers inspire?' In fact, only when we see the results of the stories can we see what people really make of them! This is the area of what we call 'people's Bible study', which happens most naturally in Base Christian Communities, in various parts of the world, now including Britain. SICEM churches are very like Base Christian Communities, and several local instances of contemporary actions coming from scripture are in the British Liberation Theology series, edited by Chris Rowland and myself.[4] The second volume, *Gospel from the City*, contains articles by SICEM colleagues Inderjit Bhogal, Jane Grinonneau, Jan Royan, Duncan Wilson and myself.[5] The third volume, *Liberation Spirituality* has Inderjit Bhogal, Jan Royan, Grace Vincent and myself.[6] All are about discipleship 'spinoffs' in our context.

Inevitably, this third question, about Gospel 'practice' today, ends with a question for every reader:

If these stories were heard to be provocative or supportive
for Gospel-like actions by these people
in these situations today,
What does this say
about the kind of people and the kind of situations
where such actions could be prepared for or awaited,
or even precipitated,
by others – including me?

# PART TWO

# PEOPLE OF SORROWS AND SURPRISES

*The Life of the Poor as the Seeds of Salvation*

*In the streets of every city, let the love of Christ be seen.*
*And then let us gladly follow, to the places he has been.*
*We will mount the steps of tower blocks, we will ride the busy train,*
*In the frailty of his body, he will walk the streets again.*

*Through the power lines of the city, let the love of Christ be heard.*
*We are speaking to the powerful, it is time to heed his word.*
*We are singing songs of justice, bringing good news to the poor,*
*In the protest of his body, he will speak for evermore.*

*To the faithful of the city, let the love of Christ be known.*
*Let us join our hands together, by whatever names we own.*
*We must celebrate our cultures, we must dance and we must sing,*
*In the sharing of his body, he will all his glory bring.*

*In the sorrow of the city, let the love of Christ be felt,*
*We are standing with the broken, and the bridges can be built.*
*We are praying for forgiveness, for the hurts that we have made,*
*In the breaking of his body, he will heal and he will save.*

*With the people of the city, let the love of Christ be shared.*
*Let us give the invitation to the feast he has prepared.*
*For his table it is open, let our hearts be open too.*
*In the loving of his body, he our cities will renew.*

David Hill

# 6

# Poor

## – and the Widow's Mite, and Levelling

*The Guardian* for 14 May 1998 contained the comments of our local MP and long time friend and supportor, David Blunkett, the Education Secretary. The political correspondent, Anne Perkins, writes:

David Blunkett, the Education Secretary, yesterday warned his own government that it risked widening divisions in society by allowing the most deprived to feel that Labour was doing nothing for them. He admitted that it was taking time for initiatives to be felt and said that last Thursday's local election turnout – well below 30 per cent in some Labour councils, including his own city of Sheffield – contrasted with the party's success in affluent areas such as Bromley and Barnet.

Mr Blunkett said the unwillingness of people to go out and vote could not be attributed to a 'culture of contentment'. 'Some of it is a bewilderment as to what is happening around them and whether the measures being taken are being felt by those for whom they are intended.' In his own city of Sheffield, he said, six secondary schools did not meet the national average for achieving five GCSEs. 'In the years ahead, we have to ensure that people hear the message – because unless they do, unless they feel part of that change, they will disengage.'

'I reject the notion that this is some sort of battleground between the worst off and the better off. It is about engaging our community with all its strengths and talents. This government will be judged by what it does for society and for

Just as God judges.

our nation as a whole. I will be judged by my constituents, by what government and what I, as an individual – including my work as a cabinet minister – do for those who are at greatest disadvantage.'

These startlingly frank comments sum up the confusion of many of us. Do we support poverty lobbies (where are they?) or go for a consensus (what is that?)? Meantime, 'top directors gave themselves pay rises of more than 26% last year – almost four times as large an increase as average profits, five times the growth of average earnings, and ten times the rate of inflation'. *The Guardian*, which gives these figures (19 July 1999), also lists 800,000 children 'due to be lifted out of poverty', plus increases in child benefit and income support for under-11s, plus tax credits. But three million children are still trapped in poverty. *The Guardian* Leader concludes:

Labour needs to set out the most fundamental welfare principle of all: what is an adequate income. This is not a technical but a political issue. No British government has ever set out a minimum acceptable standard of living, but six western nations have already done so in the last decade. The inadequacy of our current benefits can no longer be ducked.

Meantime, our witness has to be that the poor are often the seed-bearers of change. One Sunday morning at Upper Wincobank Chapel,[1] we were reading the story of the Widow's Mite in Mark 12. 41–44. We had read it over together, each member reading a verse as we usually do.

Jesus sat down opposite the Treasury, and watched the people putting money into the Treasury. Many wealthy people put in large amounts of money. A poor widow came up and put in two small copper coins, which are worth a penny.
    He called his disciples to him and said to them:
    'I'm telling you. This poor widow has put in more money

than all the rest who are giving to the Treasury. For all of them made contributions out of their affluence. But she has contributed out of her poverty. And what she put in was everything she had, all she had to live on.'

So the story was before us. I began my 'exposition'. The incident took place in the temple, in which offerings were made, of all kinds. There were large receptacles into which gifts of money could be placed. Monetary gifts were often over and above the regular gift offerings, which marked certain stages in life, or certain needs for forgiveness. So, givers of money were, in a special way, giving of themselves. However, the important thing is not the amount of money you give (I said). The important thing is what the money represents. The giving of the rich was obviously great. But then so was the wealth out of which they gave. The giving of the poor woman was obviously minuscule. But so was the wealth out of which she gave. And what she gave was all she had. So, proportionately, she gave an enormous gift, whereas the wealthy people had only given minuscule ones.

Suddenly the service erupted – as our services in SICEM quite often do.

'I can't see your problem,' said Margaret Wood. 'We saw this happen last night.'

'Oh?' said the rest of us. 'How?'

'Well,' she replied, 'It was the Annual Festival of Queens at the City Hall. All the May Queens from the different churches were all up there sitting on the platform. And our chapel's Louise was there.'

'They'd put all the May Queens from the west of Sheffield – where the rich churches are – on one side of the platform. And all the Queens from the east and north were on the other side. Our little Louise looked a bit pathetic, I must say. You all remember how we'd had to scrape around for her costume. And she looked so small beside the big girls from the west.'

'And I felt, Well, I'm glad we're here. But it's the same old thing – the west has the money, and the east hasn't.'

'But then, at the end of the evening, they started reading out the totals of money that the different churches had raised. They read out the totals for the west of the city – and they were really quite good. But then they read out the totals for the churches in the east, and they were bigger. And the people from the east all started cheering, because we'd done better. Isn't that like the widow's mite?'

Yes, we all said. That's exactly it. The poor churches are still looked down on, because they are poor. But they often give money better than the richer churches – and better not just proportionate to their incomes, but better in real terms. The Poor Widow's Story is alive and well in Wincobank – and in many a poor church in a poor neighbourhood, up and down the country.

There seem to be at least two things that have to be said about poverty from the point of view of the Bible. The first thing is that the God of the Bible is against poverty, because it represents a fundamental denial of the divine purpose to bring wholeness and justice and fulfilment to every person equally. The second thing is that we must all learn from the poor.

There is therefore a purpose of 'Levelling', of 'making things even', going on. John the Baptist in Luke 3.5 represents this dramatically:

> All low places must be filled up,
> All hills and mountains levelled off;
> Winding roads must be straightened out,
> Rough paths must be smoothed off.

'Getting even' with someone depends on who you are. For some it is clearing off old scores, paying off old debts, squaring accounts. For others, it can be grasping what others have which makes them deprived or victimized, in which case it means retaliation, revenge, 'being quits'. It appears that the God of the Bible is inordinately concerned with 'getting even'. His 'rightness' is offended when things are 'wrong'. When things are unbalanced, or unfair, or out of joint, God is concerned and offended, and seeks to bring in a more just situation. According to Luke's view, John is not the Kingdom – he is the final preparer of things prior to the Kingdom. The Kingdom itself is the activity and words of Jesus – something much more than this 'levelling off'. But the levelling off has to come first, as the prerequisite, as the proper state of affairs into which the Messiah and his special message must be brought. So, when the people said to John the Baptist, 'What are we to do then?', he said (Luke 3.11):

> Whoever has two shirts, must give one to someone without any.
> Whoever has food, must share it with others.

*Prob – equal work*

In other words, a commonwealth of equality of possessions was to be instituted, in which those who had possessions were to share them with those who had none. Everyone would thus end up with one shirt, and everyone with enough food. Doubtless, some people questioned whether this meant the complete end to all the normal economic and political arrangements of life in Palestine. But John did not conceive it so. Rather, it was to be a situation in which as far as possible, everyone would be treated the same, even if the system remained the same. Thus, when tax collectors came for baptism and asked what they were to do, John replied, 'Only collect what is legal – no more' (Luke 3. 12–13). When soldiers asked the same, he said, 'Don't extract money from anyone by force or illegally. And be content with your pay.'

Jesus was part of John's movement, but saw that it had limited results. So Jesus himself became an 'acted parable' of Kingdom 'commonness', gave up his own livelihood, lived with the poor, and invited his disciples to do the same (Mark 1. 18–20; 10. 28–31). Jesus thus pioneered God's Project of equality and sharing in his own Project and Movement.

Fundamentally, I believe that all the evidence suggests that this kind of 'radical' view is the only one which in fact deals with the present realities of poverty, and which holds out real prospects for the poor. There must be radical change – and radical change from the top, bringing people nearer to those at the bottom, and creating genuine commonness.[2]

The 1997 Methodist Report, *The Cities*, tries to utter a cry from people in the cities, appealing to people everywhere, to the politicians, and to the churches, to attend to the growing scandals of our cities, and to do something about them. The urgency of the call seems to fall on largely deaf ears. But the urgency is ever increasing. In the year 2000, more than half the world's population are now city dwellers. Cities constitute the dramatic polarizations of our time – between entrepreneurs and unemployed, between car drivers polluting inner areas and the trapped people who live there, between elite developers and decision-makers creating policies, and the ordinary people who are the victims of those policies.[3]

Can there be, we ask in the Report, cities of hope, justice and equality, genuine partnership, participation by all, genuine political accountability and long term sustainability? These are the basics of a full life, the lack of which keeps people poor, and keeps poor areas in deprivation. In the Report we oppose the 'pseudo-partnership in which the best off are outrageously well rewarded, and the worst off excluded from any share in society worthy of the meaning'. We demand realistic policies based on common action to deal with decay and demoralization, inadequate standards of living, homelessness, crime, racial attacks, unsafe no-go areas, which are the reality of city life for many. We want to combat increasing polarization by 'reconnecting wealth creation and the wider community', by 'bringing on board all sectors to regenerate from the bottom up'. AIM

Our report seeks to move beyond our 'Petition of Distress from the Cities' which a group of ministers presented to the Queen and government in 1994.[4] Our Report seeks to offer constructive suggestions for a new vision for the cities. It remains to be seen, I have to say, whether there is sufficient national will to deal with the present situation, and to start working towards that vision. 'Welfare reform' is still being debated, thought some of it has been done.

The situation gets worse by the day. As Nick Davies comments (*The Guardian*, 5 August 1998):

Out in the bleak inner city estates, in dilapidated housing, in the shelled-out schools and battered community halls, in the hidden landscape of crack houses and illegal gambling dens, in the red-light areas and on the pavements where children play, there are 10 million people who rely on a benefit which fails to provide the necessities of life and which has been cut and cut again with ruthless indifference to the welfare of those relying on it. There are 3 million others relying on earned incomes that are equally inadequate and would have been illegal had the Tories not scrapped the wages councils.

The solution to this cannot be further discipline for the poor, much less the creation of jobs – which seems less likely to happen, with present-day economics. It is hard to see how any solution or mollification to the problem of poverty can be found without some move towards equalization, some effort at levelling.

In the life of our Mission, we perhaps have begun to see a clue. All branches and congregations are not the same in capacity, resource or finance. But institutions can fundamentally change their practice by changing their intentions, their commitments. SICEM is based not on equality but on the will to share, not on all being the same, but on an intention to move towards levelling. Barry Swift, the SICEM Treasurer, writes:

Our attitude to finance is the living out of our foundation principle – the will to share. All have struggled financially for much of their lives, and continue to do so, but they are rarely disheartened. The commitment to each other is strong. If one unit cannot afford its share of the budget, other units have *always* counted the cost and found more to give out of their own poverty. The significance of the relationship is that there are no arguments – nor indeed any thought given – to 'what we get for our money'. Ministry in SICEM is not a personal chaplaincy to those within the units. Our life together is mutual support in serving others in our community in the various ways, large and small, which open up to us.

Ultimately, the 'will to share' is the only answer to poverty. The life of the poor has the seeds of salvation.

# 7

# Excluded

## – and the Guests at the Messianic Banquet

People in deprived areas are often excluded from the normal things that make life valuable. They often live isolated lives, cut off from other people, or from involvement in common activities which give meaning and richness to life, and which come from the mutuality and relatedness which social activity brings. If contemporary life is an encounter with ever-multiplying riches and variety, then deprivation means the all but complete absence of such riches and variety.

In these days, when the great and the good all talk about the evil of social exclusion, and the need for social inclusion, I often wonder whether they know what social inclusion would really mean, especially for them! Inclusion and exclusion, being brought in and being kept out, are consistent themes in Jesus' project of the Kingdom, and his stories about the Kingdom. The image for inclusiveness, for wholeness, for completeness, is often the Great Feast, or the Wedding Dinner, images of the Messianic Banquet, to which all are invited, but to which not all think it worthwhile to come. The story in Luke 14. 15–21 has become significant for us:

> One of the guests at the dinner party heard Jesus talk about the resurrection of the righteous (v. 14), so he exclaimed 'How blessed is anyone who will feast in the kingdom of God.'
>
> Jesus told him this story:
> 'A certain man was laying on a great dinner banquet, and invited many people. When it was all ready, he sent his slave to say to them, "Come, for everything is now ready." But

they all began to make excuses. One said, "I've just bought some land and must go and see it. Please accept my apologies." Another said, "I've just bought five pairs of oxen, and need to try them out. Please accept my apologies." Another said, "I've just got married, so I cannot come."

So the slave came back and told all this to his master.

Then the lord of the house became angry and said to his slave, "You go out immediately into the streets and the alleys of the city, and bring in poor people, crippled people, blind people and disabled people."

This done, the slave said, "Sir, what you ordered has been done, but there are places left still."

Then the lord said to the slave, "Go this time into the lanes and the hedges, and get hold of people and force them to come in, so that my house might be full. For I tell you, not a single one of those originally invited people shall even get a taste of my banquet."'

Jane Grinonneau tells how one night, as a Wednesday evening series of 'telling stories' at The Furnival came to an end, they took the Great Feast story of Luke 14 and acted it out.[1] A central table was set, burdened with special good things. Other tables were set more simply, as for their usual shared meal that concluded every evening's storytelling. Some of the women asked, 'Who's coming?' Jane smiled – 'I don't know.' They pressed further. 'Who is going to sit at *that* table?'

Helen Platt and Jane acted the drama with variations on the excuses. 'I'm going to wash my hair,' 'I need to tidy my room,' 'I've got a man to see and well, you know, I must see him.' After the excuses, Helen left. One woman got out of her chair and pursued her, saying it wasn't fair not to stay and eat if she had said she would. They talked about the story.

Then one woman, face set hard, became angry. Jane talked about the feast, of love and hope and relatedness in the kin-dom (Jane's word for Kingdom). The woman exploded. 'It's not bloody fair,' she said. Jane was not prepared for the outburst. 'What is not fair?,' she asked. The woman replied, this time up on her feet and shouting, 'If we could see the feast, we'd all come.' Jane concludes the story:

> There was no next sentence, no neatly packaged sentiment, nothing more said. My twisted stomach hurt, as if I had been kicked, at the agony of the insight. Those who profess to be at the table are called to make visible the feast in such a way that others are compelled to the table. We had supper – only fish and chips. But things would never be the same.

Occasionally we manifest the Great Feast. We have parties with people from all the SICEM branches coming with their 'party pieces' – like the 'WOW' Evening of January 1998, or the 'Dreams' lunch of January 1999, or the day out into the country, or the canal trip. Invariably a meal is part of the occasion.

And our places themselves become banqueting halls. One day in May 1998, as I was busy getting together an earlier version of these pages, I spent an hour with Jane on some of her stories. Coming down from the office, the smell of bacon met me. I went into the main bar, and there it was – Helen Platt and Marcus Scott (both vegans!) and Josie Stocks (now the café manager) running the café, serving bacon or egg butties, with a price list at bargain rates.

'What will you have, John?'

I looked down the list. 'I'll have the Full Monty,' I replied – bacon, sausage, egg and tomato.

As I sat down to eat my 'second breakfast', all kinds of folk from the neighbourhood were around me, talking, having cups of tea or coffee. And into this feast came Jane with two ladies from a national charity, who had been invited to come and discuss a possible grant application. Jane insisted on seeing them there. Everyone is invited to the same banquet!

Everyone has to come to the banquet. The banquet is for everyone.

When Jane started at The Furnival in September 1996, I found

myself with a 'charge' from the Gospel about Christ's message
as he comes in the city today. It's in six affirmations about
'What is not true' and 'What is true'. So much of it is about the
new future that is promised, and that really has to start now.

1. It is not true that the Kingdom of God will never come on
earth, and that we have to put up with hell on earth and wait for
heaven hereafter. This is true: Jesus says:

> The Kingdom of God is among you
> The Kingdom of God is within you (Luke 17. 21).

Our charge is: Treat everything as holy. Everything can contain
the Kingdom. Everything and everyone now are pregnant with
God.

2. It is not true that some people in the world are not worth
bothering with, and that we ought to concentrate on people of
influence and standing. This is true: Jesus says:

> I come not to call the righteous,
> But the unrighteous, the outsiders (Mark 2.17).

Our charge is: Go not only to those who need you; but to those
who need you most.

3. It is not true that some problems in the cities are insoluble,
that poverty, disadvantage, racism, discrimination are just part
of the market system, which cannot be changed. This is true:
Jesus says:

> I come that they might have life,
> And have it more abundantly (John 10.10).

Our charge is: Tend the tiniest shoots of wholeness. Never
break the bruised reeds. Love all things and all people into
abundance.

4. It is not true that we need more decision-makers,
responsible people, people of significance in the church. This is
true: Jesus says:

Unless you become as little children,
You shall not enter the Kingdom of God (Matt. 18.3).

Our charge is: Study to be among others as a child. Get going contrary movements of naivety and faith; which will judge the world and lead to the world's own liberation.

5. It is not true that numbers make a church. This is true: Jesus says:

Where two or three are gathered together in my Name
It is I myself that is presen (Matt. 18.20).

Our charge is: Hold the twos and threes as holy. They are the seed-beds of radical change. They are the nucleus of renewed community everywhere.

6. It is not true that God's Spirit is available as a spiritual enrichment to our lives and churches regardless of their obedience in terms of justice and practical righteousness. This is true: Jesus says:

God's Spirit is upon me
to preach good news to the poor
bring liberation to captives
give sight to the blinded
offer wholeness to the broken (Luke 4.18).

Our charge is: Get on with the deeds of the Kingdom. Preach good news so that the poor have good news themselves. Empower the powerless and voiceless so that they liberate themselves. Give sight to people everywhere in darkness, blinded by wealth, career, success, education. Bring wholeness to a broken creation – on the streets of every city.

One particular group of the isolated are the single parents. At Lopham Street, NCH Action for Children ran a project for single teenage mothers in our area, an involvement which they now continue at The Furnival through the developing Healthy Living Centre.

In Grimesthorpe, a young single mother had asked me to baptize her baby. I'd been round to go through the service with her. On the Sunday (it was Christmas) I preached on Matthew 1. 18–25, the story of Mary's conception of Jesus, and of Joseph, the hidden father. According to Matthew's story, Mary is made pregnant by the Holy Spirit before Joseph knows anything about it. And the fact that the angel had to plead with Joseph to go through with the marriage, and that Joseph hesitated to do so, shows that the divine conception of Mary was an 'act of God' solely related to Mary. Obviously, the birth of the Son of God would have gone ahead with or without Joseph standing by. In other words, the purpose of the conception was a conception by the unmarried young woman, a single parent. The purpose was a birth out of wedlock.

At this point, the parents and relatives wanted in on the action.

'You mean that Jesus Christ had an unmarried mother?'

'Yes, that's what the story says,' I replied.

'That's good news for the street, isn't it?' said someone.

The 'participatory sermon' continued. 'So what does this mean for the church's emphasis on the family, then?' asked someone.

'Perhaps,' I replied, 'perhaps it means that parenthood is a divine mystery, and in the will of God. And that families are also a divine mystery. But you do not necessarily get them both together.'

'That makes sense on the street,' commented another.

'At any rate,' I concluded, 'it means that God has a funny way of working with human beings. And that no one is necessarily excluded because of who or what they are – or are not. On the street it means that God's free love, God's grace, cannot ever be kept away.'

'Shall we do the baptism now?'

# 8

# Unemployed

## – and the Labourers in the Market Place

Unemployment is a major problem for us. So are underemployment, and temporary employment, and low-paid employment. Indeed, the realities of our area have imposed an equality of poverty. Older men have no jobs because they worked in industries – largely steel – which no longer need them. Women work part-time in the service sector which pays them very poor wages. Young people do not have the necessary skills for 'high tech' jobs, and drift from unemployment into training into short term jobs into unemployment again. Many are caught in the 'poverty trap', which means that they do not know whether to take a low-paid job which will merely mean that they get the same as, or even less than, what they get on 'benefits' – and have all the hassles of getting back on benefits when the job fails.

These factors have been with us throughout the 1980s and 1990s. It remains to be seen how far new policies will be able to alter them – let's hope the 'New Deal' trained youngsters actually get jobs. But these factors are the background to some attempts by us to 'send people into the vineyard' and do some work, and get some pay, during the 1980s and 1990s.

Some of the imponderables and injustices in all this, but also a keen sympathy with the unemployed, are clear in Jesus' parable of the unemployed in Matthew 20. 1–7:

> The Kingdom of heaven is like a farmer who goes out in the early morning to hire day-labourers for his vineyard. He agrees with the labourers that they work for the usual daily wages, and sends them into his vineyard.
> Then he goes out about nine o'clock and sees others stand-

ing idle in the market-place and says to them, 'You also go
out into the vineyard, and I will pay you whatever is right.' So
they go.

   Again, at noon, and again at three, he does the same.

   At five o'clock, he goes out and finds others standing
around, and he says to them, 'Why are you standing here idle
all day?' They replied, 'Because no one has hired us.' He said
to them, 'You also go into the vineyard.'

You cannot live and work in the inner city without being
aware of the people 'hanging around, standing idle in the
market place' (v. 3). At Firvale, at Spital Hill, on Verdon Street,
you can see them many days.

And you also cannot live in the inner city without being
acutely aware of all the issues of justice and fairness involved in
employment and unemployment. To 'pay someone whatever is
right' (v. 4) is the promise of all employers! But what is right?
Many around here are constantly victimized in the so-called
'jobs market'.

And you cannot live here without being exposed to the contemporary need for a 'living wage' or a 'basic income' – the
modern equivalent of the farmer in Jesus' story who 'choses to
give to the latest arrivals the same as he gives to the first' (v. 14).
And why does someone not expose the farmer's arbitrariness?
No Trades Unions here!

Clearly, community groups and churches ought to be
involved in the provision of employment, if we can be. The
problems of moving from provision of services to provision of
employment are enormous. Our only experience of it was in
1981–1988, when the ten little churches, units and house congregations were involved in the Sheffield Churches Community
Programme Agency, which employed up to 160 part-time and
full-time workers under the Manpower Services Commission
(MSC), with Ian McCullough, now the Sheffield Diocesan Faith
in the City Development Worker, as manager. One July, we had
a Day on Ministry in SICEM, and critiqued our practice. 'It is
hard to know whether in trying to respond to unemployment

we are conniving at government wickedness,' someone said. So we set down the things we gained from operating in the Community Programme Projects, and the things we lost through it.

The list went as follows:

*Advantages*
Projects
have opened our eyes to society, politics, decision-making, urban needs, people in personal need;

have produced some worthwhile things – services to people

have enabled the churches to open up to the local communities;

have provided salaries or money to do things which otherwise would not have been done;

have permitted us to provide worthwhile jobs for individuals for a year;

have meant that we focus on some specific needs for a time;

have given some people significant insights and openings into new possibilities;

have produced salaries for people who want to do a job they wouldn't otherwise be able to do;

have allowed a few people a way of keeping body and soul together while they perform or discover a personal ministry.

*Disadvantages*
However, projects
have made us into business people and employers;

become a pain and burden to us if we are landed with it forever;

mean that employed people from outside do work that ordinary members would do;

have prevented us from being fully alternative, or developing our own self-generated projects;

have meant that ultimately project-providers, not ourselves, determine what is done;

merely prop up the consumer society in which we are just kept in limbo, and we never tackle the basic issues.

With regard to projects and their relationship to ministry, there were three kinds of ministry which were named: ministry to people who come on the scheme, to give them new horizons; ministry by people on the scheme who minister to us in the church; and ministry by church people to meet needs, in any way they can. So that many and good things, and some Gospel things, got done. And many in need were helped.

In the end, we withdrew our agency from the MSC as its terms and conditions became unacceptable. But immediately we called together all our local church people who had been involved in the various community projects, and determined to carry on what we could. We formed the SICEM Community Work Committee, set up a small SICEM Community Work Trust and determined to keep going at least the two mother and toddler groups and the eight old people's lunch clubs that existed in various churches. At the same time, those who had been involved in the minibus transport which brought old people to lunch clubs, and took youngsters out on trips, formed Pitsmoor and Shiregreen Community Transport, initially as two operations, later combined. But the detailed dossiers of 1,000 housebound and sick people, whom our Care Team had been helping, could only be taken in to Redvers House, to the city Family and Community Services, where the social workers simply had to say, 'We can do nothing about them.'

The SICEM Community Work Committee has continued to meet every month or two. It consists of one or two people involved in various community projects, from each of the churches. A grant of the government's Department of Health Opportunities for Volunteering Scheme meant we could employ Alan Hindmarch as SICEM Community Work Co-ordinator from 1989 to 1993, a task then carried on by Peter Habeshaw, who continued it part-time until 1998, when Mick Todd took over.

We can keep our volunteers and our projects going, with bits of help from the local authority. And some magnificent work is done, with volunteers and 'clients' often merging together.

Moreover, in several of our branches, there have been paid jobs which local people do, though mainly part-time.

But we have been unable to provide more than a handful of paid posts, and they are all related to our projects themselves.

I have told the story of the MSC scheme in a little detail for three reasons. First, because, as a matter of historical accuracy, it is the case that the years 1983–88 were decisive ones in the life of our small churches. Partly, through the help of the Community Programme, we moved from a position of great vulnerability and insecurity, in which survival was often the name of the game, into a much more open and community-related stance. That stance, epitomized in the SICEM Community Work Committee, and championed and serviced especially by Alan Hindmarch and Peter Habeshaw, has decisively changed the character of the Mission.

The story is also important, secondly, because I am convinced that in the future we will need to remember the lessons which those years taught us. On the one hand, we must be ready to be 'taken over' by schemes as they come and go, if the aims of them are for the good of people in our area. On the other hand, we must be aware of the problems of sharing in outside-organized, government-sponsored or other schemes.

Thirdly, the story is salutary because it indicates dramatically our need for help in terms of work and employment provision. We needed our buildings as bases for the schemes. Our buildings now need to be the places not only of services to the community, but also of work and industry within the community.

How this will happen, I do not know.

Outside SICEM – or at present outside it! – one or two 'straws in the wind' are worth recording.

On 4 June 1998, I went to the launch of a campaign to set up a Sheffield Employment Bond.[1] It was organized by City Life – 'an initiative of the Relationships Foundation, tackling city poverty and unemployment'. The aim was to secure pledges from 'the more affluent end of the population' stating that they would buy Employment Bonds. Once the first £1,000,000 loans are pledged, the public and local authorities are asked to pledge a second £1,000,000. Supporters purchase zero-interest Bonds, as loans over a five-year period. A proportion of the capital is lent to North British Housing Association who use it for local housing construction and then repay the full amount plus interest. The rest of the money is used as a Social Venture Capital Fund, 'providing capital or revenue for projects for which access to conventional finance is not readily available', which will be used for new start businesses, existing small businesses, the voluntary sector and community enterprises. The Bond is now up and running.

Meanwhile, we already have a Sheffield Enterprise Agency,[2] with very wide sponsorship from the city's commercial sector and charitable trusts, 'working together to create wealth and jobs for the people of Sheffield'. And Industrial Mission in South Yorkshire has pioneered some imaginative work through the Sheffield Community Enterprise Development Unit,[3] which has developed local community projects with jobs in the nearby Darnall/Attercliffe area. It is worth quoting the Unit's purposes, which are:

1. to help a local community enterprise, a not-for-profit business which is owned and managed by local people aiming to provide a service and offer social and economic benefits for the area in which it operates;

2. to participate in the economic regeneration of Sheffield by developing existing community enterprises and assisting in the creation of new ones;

3. to work with local networks to develop an area based plan in order to create jobs and training and volunteering opportunities for the community;

4. to provide for the development of community enterprises including ongoing support with business planning, funding, management and training;

5. to give up to £5,000 and £20,000 as part of the development process.

Within SICEM, in Autumn 1999, The Furnival Burngreave Community Projects has launched Verdon Street Enterprises with schemes for launderette, nearly new clothes, and refurbished furniture, and with workshop spaces for cottage industry, based in unoccupied flats, shops and garages in the area. Write for the latest information![4]

# 9

# Immigrants

## – and the Syrophoenician Woman

Marginal areas are often the places where all kinds of people end up, who come from all kinds of different places. Our area of Pitsmoor–Burngreave is just such a cosmopolitan area. The multi-racial or multi-cultural dimension in any neighbourhood obviously makes it distinctive. There are distinctive problems to be met, certainly distinctive learnings to be gathered, and at times distinctive growths and blessings to be received. It is both the challenge and the difficulty of the situations which are at the forefront in the encounter of Jesus in a very multi-cultural situation, recorded in Mark 7. 24–30:

> Jesus set out from Galilee and went away into the country of Tyre. He got lodging in a house, and did not want anyone to know he was there. However he could not remain unnoticed. A woman who had a little daughter who was possessed by an unclean spirit immediately heard about him. She came and bowed down at his feet. Now the woman was a Gentile, a native of Syrophoenicia. She begged him to cast the demon out from her daughter.
>
> Jesus said to her, 'We have to feed the children first. We can't take the food away from the children and give it to the dogs'.
>
> But she answered, 'Sir, indeed. But the crumbs the children drop get eaten under the table by the dogs'.
>
> Then he said, 'All right – for saying that, you can go in peace. The demon has left your daughter.' So she went home, and found the child lying on the bed, the demon gone.

It is a highly debatable story. It doesn't show Jesus up in a good light, as he apparently has to be persuaded into healing the woman's daughter, against his better judgment, and as a result of the woman's witty reply, exposing his narrowness. But it also shows Jesus in a good light, as being prepared to act mercifully toward a Gentile although his convictions were against it. Jesus is not always right. Or, perhaps, in order to get to being right, he has to be prepared to venture himself in a spontaneous response that turns out to be wrong! But his comment about 'dogs' looks distinctly racist!

I like the story, because it indicates so well the mixed feelings of people in mixed race areas. Jesus, a Jew, has run away from his own people, and temporarily forgotten that there are people in the foreign place to whom he is a foreigner, so he cannot act on the natural responses he could get away with at home. He has perhaps to face the fact that something which would not have been asked of him in Galilee can legitimately be asked of him in Tyre. The passage is tricky and difficult, whichever way you read it. But I am glad that it is there, because it makes it possible for us to feel not too bad about our own surviving bits of 'racism', and our own ambiguity when caught off our guard.

Living in a multi-racial area has many pains and many pleasures – which means mixed feelings, to put it mildly! It is not easy suddenly to find yourself surrounded by people of a different race or colour, with a totally different world view – Jesus among Gentiles, Pitsmoor people among Muslims. Inderjit Bhogal has well described the feelings of the surviving whites in our situation. In our volume of essays, *Gospel from the City*, he calls it 'grieving'.

There are people who 'lament and despair' the fact of plural Britain. The despair is not unlike the despair of bereavement. The concerns of those who feel 'British Culture' is being eroded do need attention too. The sense of loss and bereavement needs to be recognized as such and to be tackled imaginatively if we are to come to terms adequately with our plural context. If we don't, some hurts will remain unhealed, and there will always be bitter and resentful racists who will carry an unresolved and dangerous anger within them which will have damaging effects upon us all.[1]

Happily, many of us feel that there are more gains than losses in multi-racial Pitsmoor and Burngreave. We may not be desperately good at what more enlightened suburbanites call 'multi-faith dialogue', but we live alongside each other with tolerance, amusement, mutual curiosity and occasionally common endeavour. The situation in which we live is odd and novel, but rarely vicious. We get used to each other, and to curious experiences – like my own, of writing these words about Christianity, while on the other side of the wall behind my desk, twenty or twenty-five Muslim children are reciting the Koran in the house next door, being used as a temporary Mosque.

A greater problem is felt by the non-local whites. Perhaps had Jesus as a Jew lived in Tyre, he would have been more accustomed to Gentile, non-Jewish people – though, frankly, Galilee itself was a multi-national, multi-faith area. Certainly, the white ex-residents take a dim view of inner city Pitsmoor now. 'Why do you stay?', they ask. Racism, or incipient racism, or institutionalized racism (I write after the Lawrence report) are far more likely to be present in those who do not live alongside people of other races. Indeed, were they willing to do so, there is much that they could learn from us, who live daily with those of other races.

Some afternoons, I used to meet my grandson, Reuben, from the local school. His father, Chris, and our two other children, also went to Firs Hill Primary and Junior School, as did many residents up and down Abbeyfield Road. Over the years, the school has become more and more non-white – firstly mainly Afro-Caribbean, now mainly Pakistani and Bangladeshi. The school battles at the bottom of the attainments league. The Christmas nativity play is played mainly by non-whites, Muslims – for Jesus, of course, is also in the Koran.

Inderjit takes his children to the same school. He describes his experience thus:

On week day mornings during school term, I like to walk with our two children, Liamarjit aged 8 and Anjuli aged 6, to school. At about 8.45 am the local streets are crowded with other parents, guardians and children. We reflect the community. We are black, Asian, white, young, middle aged, old. At one point on the journey, many of us have to cross a busy through road, Barnsley Road. At 8.45 am, the cars and buses and trucks are bumper to bumper both ways. Cyclists who brave the road wear masks to cope with all the fumes. A lollipop lady assists those who wish to cross the road.

As we wait at the pelican crossing, I look round and feel a thrill at the multi-cultural, multi-coloured, multi-religious group of women, men, boys and girls around me. In the midst of all the local concerns related to the many poor, the many religions, the many trees; in the midst of all the struggle in life we represent, we are a sign of the Kingdom of God which Jesus said is 'in the midst of you'. And I rejoice and give thanks to God.

As I look around, I see also the faces of people looking out of buses and cars at us. Sometimes as they speed on, people turn their faces in the vehicles to look at us. But the looks are depressing. The faces show a sense of sheer resentment – the faces say something like: 'I used to live there. Pitsmoor was a good place. Now its over-ridden by all these "foreigners".'
And they pass through. That's all they do now . . . pass through – to town, to work, to homes elsewhere. They do not share my sense of delight at what I see. They only seem to deplore what they see. I want more people to rejoice with me, to see in the city signs of the New Jerusalem, the Kingdom of God.[2]

According to Jesus in Luke 13. 29–30, the vision of the Kingdom of God is one where 'People will come from the east and the west, the north and the south, and will eat in the Kingdom of God. Indeed, some who are last will be first, and some who are first will be last.' Our practice in SICEM suggests that, despite all the difficulties, it is possible for all people, in

a natural and human way, to move from fear and grieving.
The way is that of mutuality, tentative friendships and occasionally sharing common projects. Inderjit says we need three
things:

1. To meet with those who are different from us for dialogue
and to form relationships of mutual trust and respect on the
basis of which we can learn from, and about, each other, and
work together for the common good;

2. To move from white, middle-class, male-oriented perspectives of our concerns towards those that encompass larger
boundaries of colours, cultures, creeds, genders, geographies
and abilities;

3. To move from an absolutizing and supremacy of white
Eurocentric and British Culture towards a pluralism that recog-
nizes, respects and values other human cultures as contributing
to the wholeness of being human.[3]

So far, our journey has not led us very far. We have occasional sessions at UTU when local Muslims come to speak and
discuss. There was a Christian-Muslim Mothers and Toddler
Group at St James for many years. Their premises were used for
a while for Koran instruction to Muslim boys. In the wider
society, there is more working together – in the local schools, in
the community centre, in the political parties, and above all in
the new Burngreave Community Action Forum, which brought
all local community groups together to assemble our bid for
Single Regeneration Budget money, and whose Chairperson is
my near neighbour, Mohammed Iqbal, a local Muslim Community leader and Adult Education Lecturer.[4]

The reality seems to be that as far as we as disciples of Christ
are concerned, we are accepted as neighbours and at times
fellow-workers. Our churches, meantime, are welcomed by our
Muslim neighbours as places of religious observance and
religious discipline. Occasionally, as during the Iraq-Kuwait
war, groups of church women and Muslim women meet in each
others' homes for prayer. There is a small Sheffield Muslim–
Christian Society which meets in members' homes. In a sense,
the presence of non-Christian neighbours in some strength

enforces what might be called the specifically religious aspects of Christianity.

We Christians, after all, are respected by Muslims in the same way as Jews are respected by Christians. But with the same confused sense of disappointment, 'How is it that the Jews never came to recognize Jesus, the next revelation?', we Christians ask. 'How is it that the Christians never came to recognize Muhammad, the next revelation?' our Muslim neighbours ask. Of course, conversions are not the point. As few Christians convert 'back' to Judaism as do Muslims convert 'back' to Christianity. To expect Muslims to convert to Christianity is like expecting Christians to convert to Judaism.

But perhaps a few modest and human things like these are significant in our increasingly polarized and ghettoized world. Perhaps such gentle and tentative holding out of hands is the acceptable foretaste of those coming with all their strangeness (ourselves included!) from east and west and south and north into the Kingdom of God – in which all are strangers, but none are foreigners!

# 10

# Teenagers

## – and the Bravado of James and John

I saw *The Full Monty* in New York, with Geoff Curtiss, a long-time UTU colleague there. I found great difficulty with it. It was too near to home. Was I really watching a film? Next day, staying with our son James there, I saw it again with him. 'It's the Sheffield you committed yourself to, Dad. It's the Sheffield I left behind,' he said.

In *The Sheffield Telegraph*, there was a great debate about 'the harm it's doing to Sheffield as a go-ahead, modern city'. But they were wrong, I think. I applauded it because of the good it's doing to people all over the world who are faced similarly with the tragi-comedy of the useless, pathetic males discarded by progress. It could have been filmed anywhere in the world. But it needed a locality to make it real – like the Incarnation in Nazareth. You can only see it everywhere when you've seen it somewhere.

The hero to me was the lad, Nathan, played by William Snape. He's on the street today as much as his pathetic, bravado dad, Gaz. He's still following his dad around, doing nothing, avoiding trouble, unable to break free. But then suddenly he becomes the saviour, when he offers his £100 savings to finance the booking of the hall for the show. He's the miracle, isn't he? I think they call it faith. Or madness. Or just standing beside those with no standing. Which is faith.

It's the life together, the corporate bravado, of the six men who end up putting on the show which fascinates me. They get together for their project by the oddest of means. They have little in common except desperation to do something. They are drawn into the show they have to put on by a kind of mutual daring. Gaz – the Peter of the group? – is the first to deny the cause, forced back in by his son – the saviour again! – at the last minute.

To me, it's all very like the Gospel picture of the group of disciples with Jesus. Their purpose and their names are in Mark 3. 14–19:

> Jesus appointed twelve, to be his companions, whom he could send out to proclaim good news and to have authority to cast out the demons.
> So he appointed the twelve:
> Simon, whom he called 'Peter',
> James son of Zebedee and his brother John, whom he called 'Boanerges', 'Sons of Thunder'.
> Plus Andrew, Philip, Bartholomew, Matthew, Thomas, James son of Alphaeus, Thaddaeus, Simon the Canaanean, and Judas Iscariot who betrayed him.

Mark's Gospel traces their story. At the beginning, there are only five of them. Simon and Andrew, James and John (1. 29), then joined by Levi (2. 14). The five are not happy to answer questions (2. 16–17). But they put on an agreed common front, eating and drinking to show they are different from other religious groups who are fasting (2. 18 – 20), or rubbing corn in their hands as a demonstration that their Kingdom life supercedes the old Sabbath regulations (2. 23–27), or, a bit later, eating with unwashed hands to show that the old traditions are hypocritical (7. 1–7). These are clearly provocative acts by disciples who want to 'make a point' through symbolic acts or acted parables – corporate bravado!

The disciples are acting out a new found freedom and creativity. They are Friends of Jesus the Bridegroom (2. 18–20), they are the New Wineskins for the New Wine of the Kingdom (2. 21–23), they are the contemporary equivalent of the raucous, law-breaking gang who went about with David (2. 23–28). They are the Kids of the Kingdom (10. 24), the Last who are now First (10. 31), Slaves who are really Lords (10. 41–45). Like the six Sheffielders who suddenly become stars!

James and John might well have been teenagers, I believe. Their father, who was with them in the boat (1. 19), might well have been only in his thirties or forties, as he was presumably young enough to carry on the fishing business without his sons. The nickname Boanerges, which Jesus gave the two (3. 17), which Mark translates 'Sons of Thunder', would fit a couple of rowdy teenagers more than it would two grown men.

Again, John seems quite willing to blurt out what the others were not so ready to admit (9. 38). And, above all, it is James and John who come to Jesus saying, 'We want you to do for us whatever we ask' (10. 35), and who naively answer 'Yes, we can', when asked if they can share Jesus' coming passion (10. 39). Again, the anger of the others against them (10. 41) might indicate jealousy at younger favourites, or just superiority at teenage pushers.

Luke and Matthew add to this picture of Mark. It is James and John who offer to call down fire from heaven to consume an unreceptive village (Luke 9. 52). Matthew's story – 'the mother of the sons of Zebedee came to him, and knelt and begged a favour' (Matt. 20. 20), that 'these two sons of mine' will have special places (Matt. 20. 21) – would be more credible if the sons were teenagers. Few mothers would make such a request for grown-up sons. If this is right, then Jesus chose to bring two young men into his closest group, as it is Peter, James and John who accompany Jesus at crucial points (Mark 5. 37; 9.2; 14.33).

If two of the disciples were teenagers, conceivably others might have been also. Clearly, Peter is a married man (Mark 1. 30), and has at least some of the house, brothers, sisters, mother, father, children and property which he 'leaves behind' (10. 29). And Levi has a business and a house (2. 13–15). The ages and situations of the others is harder to guess.

But, regardless of this uncertainty as to their ages, the disciples seem to have acted like teenagers, sometimes intentionally, sometimes not. Jesus calls them 'little ones', 'children', 'last ones', 'least ones', 'servants', 'slaves'. They had left behind everything and become unemployed for the sake of Jesus'

Project. They had thrown in their lot with a leader who led them they knew not where, and said it would all end in tears.

The tragi-comedy of desperate no-gooders suddenly faced with a chance to be and do something significant is the story of the six in *The Full Monty*, and the twelve in the Gospels. It's tragic because it is an apparently hopeless project; and because they are people who have little to give, disregarded by the rich and powerful, despised and rejected by other people. It's comic because the six and the twelve put up shows against the authorities, are ridiculed by relatives and friends, and have to stick at their One Hope through thick and thin. The six make it in the end. The twelve run away from it in the end.

On the streets of the cities now, desperados and misfits, job-dodgers and runaways, deceivers and betrayers, pushers and braggards get together with their frail, unbelievable projects. Let them know that they have fellowship with would-be actors (one only got £13,500 for his part!) who unexpectedly launched a £1,000,000 box office success. Let them know that they also have 'blood brothers' who clambered behind Jesus, doing bits of his thing, and becoming in the end a corporate new humanity – a new humanity still being constantly reborn.

And, of course, both the six and the twelve are saved by a young lad. The £100 savings account has its precursor in the lad who came to the rescue of the beleaguered disciples. 'You give them something to eat,' a somewhat unreasonable Jesus had told his disciples when they asked him to solve the hunger of the five thousand (Mark 6. 37). The saviour was 'a young lad here, who has five barley loaves and two fishes', according to John's Gospel (John 6. 8). And that was enough. The gang was saved at the post by a young lad giving all he had.

The mystery of redemption is still alive and well on the streets of the city. We can sometimes embody it. Sometimes we just have to wait for it.

In January 1998, we all celebrated the opening of a new project at The Furnival, the Cellar Project. Invited guests and locals went together downstairs into the basement, where an enormous transformation had taken place. Sister Una Burke, an RC sister of the Holy Union of Sisters (LSU), who had moved into the area 'in faith' with a colleague, Sister Pat Daley, only two years before, has been appointed the part-time worker.

The Cellar Project is designed to do something for excluded and truanting young people of the area. Within the total Pye Bank/Woodside population of 2,523, there are 688 under eighteen years. The teenagers attend two secondary schools, which come bottom of the LEA's performance league tables. Only 10% achieve five or more GCSE grades A–C, the Sheffield average being 37.2%. In January 1997, there were twenty-eight children permanently excluded from these and other local secondary schools who had not been placed, out of the city total of ninety-nine. Two hundred and fifty-two students attended these schools less than 50% of the time throughout the year 95/96. Meantime, the drug-dependency culture grows. Drugs and alcohol are related to most of the crime in the area, we are told, as are fights on the streets. We now produce new generations containing the seeds of today's tragedies. Not AIDS, but drugs is the main factor. In the first six months of 1998, there were twenty-eight babies born in Sheffield to heroin-dependent parents, babies who are now heroin-dependent.

What can be done? At least, set up a sign of hope, sow seeds of radically different ways! Incredibly within this context, the 'Aims and Objectives of the Cellar Project' are stated as blithely as you will – (a) to encourage and equip disaffected young people for re-entry into main-stream opportunities for education and employment; (b) to provide opportunities for parents to increase their understanding of their children's needs and to develop skills in meeting them; (c) to provide a safe, hospitable space for young people.

The Project stated its policies as to provide the local groups of young people and teenagers currently on the streets with a safe alternative venue at least four nights a week (7 pm–10 pm); to facilitate opportunities for social interaction, activities and health education for young people; to explore with educational institutions ways of enabling young people excluded from the processes of education, skill development and employment, to re-enter these processes with a conviction of self-worth, potential and hope for the future; to complement the limited provision made by the city in this area, working in partnership with other providers e.g. Recreation Centre and Youth Service locally; and to develop within the Cellar complex the integral garage space as a skills development unit for young people/parents/local residents, with the possibility, for example, of recycling furniture. Most of this is now up and running.

The redesigned cellar comprises three main spaces. Workshop 1: A social space. This is a 'common room' space, equipped with easy chairs, stereo, tea and coffee facilities, microwave, games, suitable for small-group activities and creative work. There is also a small quiet room for one-to-one counselling. Workshop 2: A technical workshop, housing technical equipment for the development of practical and vocational skills, e.g. computer equipment, sewing machines, video equipment. Workshop 3: A practical workshop designed for the development of practical skills, such as home maintenance, furniture repairs, decorating, and equipped with tools, workbench etc.

It is hoped that The Furnival Cellar Project can 'rescue' some young people from a downward spiral, and help them to believe in their own success in learning. The intention is to motivate them to return to mainstream education opportunities, or to training or work, with changed attitudes and hope for the future.

Such, at any rate, is one more 'seed' for the future, to be thrown in alongside *The Full Monty* culture. Not, I hope to extinguish it, but to help bring it again to life and extend its potential for hope and salvation.

How far the Cellar Project can affect the local culture of teenage exclusion remains to be seen. It will be, like all our efforts, one small piece of work which will significantly help a few, vulnerable people. Hopefully it will be a seed which can be multiplied elsewhere.

From March 1998, there have been young people using the Cellar. But there are still more young people outside, on the street, talking and roaming about, getting into fights, drifting into drugs, getting pregnant. Josie Stocks and a few others meet them and listen to them. And, month by month and day by day, The Furnival workers and members pick up opportunities and try them. Some fail. But the message gets out: You are accepted. And you have potential.

# 11

# Kids

## – and Who is the Greatest in God's Kingdom

'The kids are awful.' 'The kids are magic.' Both comments are heard frequently in the inner city. Kids are both an ever-present problem, and at times an ever-present plus.

The numbers of children in our areas vary as different generations grow up. Estates built in the 1930s, which for years have had elderly populations, now have young families and children. In the 1980s Shiregreen URC had opened its doors in service to the elderly people who by then were almost the entire local community. But in the 1990s, the situation has changed, as the older people have died or moved into care. Suddenly the estate seems full of children again, and they seem to the older local residents to be less cared for, and more troublesome. The council and its housing department, the police and other agencies, are beginning to co-operate and intervene to prevent any further deterioration, and new attempts by them to create community structures, such as Capital Challenge, are depending heavily on the contribution that Shiregreen URC, among others, is making to the development of a sense of belonging for new families on the estate. An education survey showed that in some of the area's schools, 57% of the children were receiving free school meals, and a more recent survey indicates an even higher percentage. The unemployment indicators, lone-parent numbers, and similar data all point to the depth of deprivation which has been experienced by people over the last ten years.

So, Shiregreen URC began to examine itself. The three old people's lunch clubs were doing a magnificent job, and needed to continue. But now the church as a whole began to learn some new things. Mark 10. 13–16, where Jesus' ministry to children is described, became a key passage to them.

> The people were bringing little children to Jesus, in order that he might lay his hands on them. And the disciples told them off for it.
>
> But when Jesus noticed what was happening, he was angry and said to the disciples: 'You must let little children come to me. You must not prevent them. For it is to such as they that the Kingdom of God belongs.'
>
> 'Honestly, I'm telling you, anybody who does not receive the Kingdom of God as a little child, will never get into it.'
>
> And he took them up in his arms, and laid his hands on them, and gave them a blessing.

Ian Lucraft reports on a discussion in the service on a Sunday in May 1998. The members had been invited to share together the Gospel passages that they felt resonated with their feeling about the life of Shiregreen. Ian had asked them to think about it during the preceding week.

The ideas shared by various people included the following, though some were more personal ideas than reflections of the church's ethos:

*The least of these*   We apply this to all kinds of people, seeing and serving Jesus in our daily life

*Seek and knock*   We're on a journey and doors are opening when we knock.

*Love one another*   We're a group trying to do the work of Christ.

*God is my refuge and strength*   We experience this on some occasions, for example when in hospital.

*A place of forgiveness*   Shiregreen as a place of forgiveness, not just saying OK, but welcoming the outcast back in.

*Martha and Mary*   Some felt like Martha that they worked hard, but wanted some of the action at the front of the house, in worship or public occasions.

*Loving Father/Prodigal Son*   We try to be open and utterly loving.

*Elder brother*   We are also protective of what we have.

The congregation went on to think of how 'Let the children come unto me' has been their theme. They looked at the upside down nature of the world Jesus was portraying in the passages leading up to the stories about the children. Ian quoted a list of Markan paradoxes, and the congregation concluded that life with the children meant:

thinking things differently
spending time with them
learning their names
asking how they see the church
asking what they want to do
learning new skills with them

Ian concludes

Then we reflected that two key stories are about receiving Christ in the children, and approaching the present Kingdom in a childlike manner of openness, enthusiasm, in an uncomplicated manner. It is not that there aren't difficult matters with which to struggle, but with the children we see the important issues of relationships, care and support. We are asked to share Christ's love in that open unrestricted and childlike way.

The background indicates the long and careful process the church had gone through prior to this. In 1993, a small group of unaccompanied children had begun to join regularly for worship on Sunday mornings. Sundays needed a 'rethink' and a number of people (about half the adult congregation) offered to share the work in Junior Church on a rota system. They were also concerned that as a church they offered only a Girls' Brigade during the midweek – nothing for the many boys on the estate, or indeed for the girls who didn't want Girls' Brigade. Everyone felt that the children and young people they had come to know – and those who were out there and they didn't yet know – should have the opportunity to meet together during the week in some sort of club activity.

So, Duncan Wilson worked with the members to create the Children and Families Project. The aims of the project were:

to provide a lively, relevant, imaginative and caring ministry to young people;
to demonstrate the congregation's faith and share its vision;
to grow as a centre of community;
to engage in common enterprise with the local community;
to enlarge the worshipping congregation;
to express the presence of Jesus Christ;
to fulfil the promise made to children and families at the sacrament of baptism.

The project was launched in September 1994 and a church member, Gwen Smithies, gave up her teaching job and became project co-ordinator. In their 1997–98 Report, the project secretary, Ian Lucraft, and the co-ordinator, Gwen Smithies, write:

We encouraged parent involvement, and immediately offered a basic training programme. We now have a committed group of parents who are part of our church family and share and take responsibility throughout the week. The Sheffield College, Sheffield City Council Department of Employment and Economic Development, the Pre-School Learning Alliance, and the Sheffield Young Children's Services were called upon to deliver (and fund – thankfully), a number of courses to be held on site at 'Shiregreen', as well as training programmes delivered by the project co-ordinator. A number of the workers attended the City and Guilds course in 'Playwork' which was delivered at Shiregreen by the Sheffield College, and our church was used as the examination centre.

Many things happen at Shiregreen. It's a busy, bustling place most of the time. Fun, friendship and commitment (and occasionally great big dollops of stress) are rarely off the menu, though that's not to say life is easy for many of us. What is always on the menu, is that we care, and people are our priority.

Perhaps to sum up and reflect, we remember that our project began with a very small number of children in mind. We continue to thank God for kids. We hope and pray that we might have foresight to understand and keep in touch with the needs of our young people as they are faced with life's tough decisions and difficulties. Some would say their needs are just as important as ours. *We* might say their needs are *more* important than ours.

Currently, the project has a variety of activities: – under 11s club, music sessions, over 11s club, summer playscheme, residentials, parent's support group, parents and toddlers, links with other groups, training and development, craft sessions, computer courses. The Project Three Year Report 1994–97 highlights two elements as especially important. First, the development of a Learning Centre, with a wide range of personal development opportunities, offers a vision of a new centre in the areas for growth and development. Second, the Parents' Support and Development Group has been a powerhouse of ideas and activity for the project, creating and facilitating new work. Several of the parents have become firm friends as well as fellow workers. One of the fathers, Mick, writes in the Report:

I came along to pick up my kids one evening, and to my surprise have been attending on a regular basis ever since. I have held baking sessions with the children to prove that a man can bake just as well as a woman. I have been abseiling, canoeing, attended football matches, pantomimes and various other craft evenings and weekends. Now, along with my wife, I help to run the small, but successful, tuck shop for the children.

The group is a place where knowledge and expertise is given and received on a free basis – although I have been known to bake a cake in return for a pencil case made by another parent – a cabinet maker. I have found the activities run by the project to be a great source of help and support together with the friendships we share, and new skills we have developed. My next challenge is to teach Gwen to make a decent cup of tea!

When I had drafted this chapter, I showed it to Gwen Smithies, and asked her to add something from her experience. This is what she wrote:

Perhaps working alongside children has given us the opportunity to share their world, to 'get real' and to face the problems that they have to deal with every day.

As a group of people involved in many very different midweek activities one of the most powerful effects that has happened is that we have learned totally to share our resources with each other. This is something which I know does not happen in many of our churches – when cupboards are locked and each unit keeps their own tea/coffee/pens/paper/toys etc. Just as the boy in John 6.8 'saved the day' and seemingly willingly shared all he had, our experience of the children is that their openness and willingness to share had a reciprocal effect on us. If we now trust each other to share our resources in our own church, then we might begin to share with our more distant neighbours.

Jesus' instruction to be 'dressed for action, with lamps already lit', in Luke 12. 35–40, sums up working with children, in that the unexpected is always close by – the unexpected volunteer; the unexpected situation; the unexpected offer; the unexpected friendship. Be ready for whatever! Set nothing in concrete! Be prepared to listen and adapt and change. By creating a safe and welcoming place for children, we also created a hospitable place for their parents to 'feel safe' too.

Today, Shiregreen's minister, Janet Lees, and the congregation together announce to all the youngsters and families who come for baptism:

> Welcome to our church!
> We hope you will soon feel part of our church family.
> We have gifts, friendship and love to share with you.
> Please share with us and be our sister/brother in God's family.
> We know you can make new friends here –
> we know because we have all made new friends here
> and we try to love and care for each other as Jesus asked us to.
> So, come, play, have fun, learn and let us all grow together
> And may you always know God's love.

The kids have found a second home![1]

# 12

# Handicapped

---

## – and Who to Invite for Dinner

The inner city has come to be the place where all the people with any kind of handicap or disadvantage gather together – or are thrust together by the 'care in the community' policies. So much so that at times we have had to shout to the Council, 'Enough is enough. Don't send any more.'

In the midst of this feeling of being used to compensate for the victimization and exclusion by the rest of society, we still have to be neighbours to all who come, especially those least able to care for themselves – the poor, the crippled, the lame and the blind, as Jesus called them – those with any kind of handicap. The story which Jesus told in Luke 14. 12–14 has been important for us.

Jesus said to his host at the dinner,

'When you are giving a lunch or a dinner,
You shouldn't invite
your friends, brothers, relations
or rich neighbours. – They will
only invite you back and you will be repaid.

No. When you are giving a banquet,
You should invite
poor, crippled, lame and blind people.
Then you will be blessed.
They cannot invite you back,
but you will be repaid
at the resurrection of the righteous.'

Since November 1991, the Burngreave Monday Lunch Club has taken place each week. It was started and is now co-ordinated by Jan Royan and Iain Cloke. Jan is a member of the St Catherine's RC Presbytery Community opposite Pitsmoor Methodist Church, where the Club meets. Iain Cloke is a schoolteacher and a SICEM Methodist Circuit Steward. Both had just completed the UTU Study Year, 1990–91. Jan now co-ordinates the Personal Theology and Mission module of the Study Year and Iain is active on the UTU Committee.

The Monday Lunch Club is for people with special needs, or learning disabilities, or what used to be called mental handicap. The Pitsmoor church became aware of the increasing number of such people around us, as the government policy of 'care in the community' meant that the local authority bought and equipped several old houses in our area, as they were, of course, cheaper to buy than houses in more prosperous areas. However, the authorities had not made sufficient social provision for them, and Jan and Iain felt the call to try to make good this deficiency.

The Club has a core of seven committed volunteers and up to twenty-five members with learning disabilities. It meets every Monday at Pitsmoor Methodist church hall, opening at 8.45 am and officially closing at 2pm. The Club includes games, artwork, occasional cooking, and a lot of talking, with a snack-style lunch served around midday. They also have several out-ings a year, which have included a picnic, trips to various parks, centres and open farms, a barbecue, an annual pantomime and a Christmas party. Birthdays are always celebrated, and at least half the members stay for the quarterly Lunch Club meeting and participate in decision-making. Everyone including relatives, carers, staff from the various residential homes and members of the Social Services is invited to the AGM which is held in May after lunch.

Jan comments:

I consider that we were fortunate in the way in which the Club has evolved. None of the volunteer helpers has had any training to work with people with learning difficulties, and to begin with we actually had a higher number of volunteers than we had members. Gradually the numbers of people attending with learning disabilities has grown, and we now have clients with little or no speech, some with physical as well as mental handicap, and some with behavioural problems. Because of our slow evolution, and the growing commitment of a much smaller group of volunteers, we have grown more confident in dealing with a wider diversity of handicap, and have developed a more individual way of relating to each of our people. Personal friendships have been formed; members living on their own or with carers and relatives are involved with volunteers in other activities in the community outside the Lunch Club. These include barn dances, coach trips, parties, walks, bingo and discos. After four years of taking small groups away for a weekend's holiday, ties of shared memories and a lot of fun are formed.

Various elements have been fundamental
  1. Creating space and opportunities for each person to fulfil his/her potential;
  2. Supporting independent risk-assessed activity;
  3. Involving as many people as possible at each stage;
  4. Listening attentively and observing sensitively the voiced and unvoiced emotions and needs of our members, and responding where we are able to, passing our observations on to appropriate people;
  5. Building up a community of deep friendship, love and commitment to each other, where joys and sorrows are shared;
  6. Exploring ways in which carers of our members and volunteers in the Lunch Club can form a partnership in which our members' interests are promoted.

Jan wrote a brilliant 8,000-word essay on 'Constructing a Theology of Liberation for Burngreave Monday Lunch Club', for a course which I tutored in Autumn 1997 at the Hallam Pastoral Centre. In it, she invented her own methodology or 'hermeneutical circle',[1] as it is called.

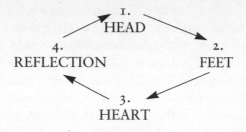

Jan describes the four stages thus:

The Head stage is the preliminary stage where all the questions are asked before the actual setting up of the Lunch Club: Why do we need a Lunch Club? Where will it be held? What will it include? For whom will it be run? To whom will we be responsible? How will it operate, be managed? With whom will we run it?

The Feet stage is the practical action; the actual putting into practice of the decisions made at the Head stage.

The Heart stage is the most difficult stage to explain. For me it happened when I realized that involvement in the Lunch Club was no longer a duty but had become a whole-hearted commitment to each other, when an option for the handicapped was made.

Finally, the Reflection stage. This is in part what happens at our quarterly Lunch Club meetings. More often it happens during unplanned and spontaneous conversations with volunteers and particularly between Iain Cloke and myself. More specifically, writing this essay has given me the space and time to reflect on the meaning of the Lunch Club in my life and those of its users.

You do not need to start with the head, comments Jan. And you do not need to have the four elements in the same order – but they all need to be involved somewhere.

The key to the Club is the word of Jesus – 'I am come that they might have life, and have it to the full' (John 10.10). How such people can have life to the full is a constant concern. Of the twenty-five current members, fifteen live in some form of permanent residential home, nine with relatives and carers, and one lives on her own with a full-time social worker. Says Jan, 'It seems to me that the biggest hurdle that many handicapped people have to overcome is that of being treated as passive objects. In this aspect they are like the poor. Because people are poor or handicapped, they can be treated with contempt and dismissed as being incapable of making any decisions for themselves.' Their 'fullness of life', or their 'liberation', is often in being awakened from passivity into action, from being objects to being subjects, from being over-protected to being allowed to take risks, from being always 'done to' to being expected to do a few things for themselves.

One of the most rewarding and encouraging parts of the Lunch Club is seeing the progress and confidence that slowly gets built up – for volunteers as well as members. An example is in watching someone who in the past could not count the spots on the dominoes now playing with confidence, or helping a less able member to play. There are numerous tasks carried out by members each Monday to make the Club run smoothly – tasks usually done not because they have been asked to do them, but because a member, seeing a need, has responded creatively to it.

Jan concludes:

For our people to become agents of their own liberation, subjects not objects, we need to recognize their right to be such agents, such subjects. We, as volunteers, have to own how often we are fulfilling our own needs when we treat members as passive objects, and how much easier it is to dominate a passive person than an active one. In creating an environment where opportunities frequently exist for awakening and stimulating potential, where effort is rewarded as much as success, and where creativity and cooperation and laughter are part of our regular Lunch Clubs, then we all – volunteers just as much as members – will hopefully become agents of our own liberation.

Duncan Wilson, who supported and worked with the Club until his departure in February 1997, writes:

At one level members are able to explore their abilities and discover new or existing gifts. They are free to be creative. At another level, however, is the acknowledgment that each individual is a person, however damaged mentally or physically, free to take part and to decide for oneself, to take charge, even to establish a little of one's own 'domain'. It is the liberty to volunteer one's own interest and initiate one's own attachments and relationships. There is no 'tyranny' of expectations designed to make life smooth for the operation of the institution.

The significance of all this in terms of Gospel practice, Gospel community, and Gospel spirituality become clear in the last part of Jan's four-point circle – reflection. Says Jan: 'Spirituality is part of the Lunch Club life. It is integral, but in the earthed, often messy and noisy reality of what we do. God's spirit has been leading us silently and unobtrusively.'

There are three elements in that spirituality. 1. Reciprocity. 'Our members may be in need of help to make drinks, to write cards or play dominoes, but in their transparency and openness, their lack of masks, they show us how to be our authentic selves. Our members are not judgmental about us as volunteers – although they can sometimes show us when we are wrong – and they are faithful in their love to us.' 2. Fidelity to the real. 'Acknowledging our departure from the real is never easy, but I believe it to be part of our Lunch Club spirituality. Somehow there is a bonding between the commitment of the heart, fidelity to the real and the work of the Spirit.' 3. Costly love. 'Being with people with learning disabilities forces us off our pedestals; forces us to recognize our own difficulties in loving. Without this costly love which shows us how to respect those who are not generally respected in society, and also how to respect the dark and hidden sides of ourselves, there can be no genuine spirituality.'

So the Lunch Club workers discover that they have been blessed by what they receive from those who they thought had nothing to give. Whatever else can be said of the members of the Monday Lunch Club, they cannot invite the lunch-givers back – which seems to be the crucial characteristic of the poor, crippled, lame and blind people in Luke 14. 12–14. They have no homes where lunch-dates can be extended. So you cannot be repaid in the same way as your friends, brothers, relatives, or rich neighbours will repay your invitation. Jesus in Luke says that those who are hosts to the handicapped will be repaid at the resurrection of the righteous (v. 14). But Luke has two places where there are repayments. One is hereafter. But the other is the community of the heart, here and now, the community of the Kingdom-celebrators, who discover that it is more blessed to give than to receive.

Initially, Iain and Jan confess that they wanted to do something for adults with learning disabilities in the area. Little did they dream that their reward would come so soon! In fact, Jan wonders if Jesus, too, knew that if the Pharisee followed his injunction, his whole world would be turned upside down – and blessings would be heaped on his head. For that has been their experience at Monday Lunch Club. Jan says:

> We thought we were proclaiming the Kingdom to our members, but it is they who proclaim it to us. Through their joy, love and commitment, we are healed and made whole. In our desire to enable them to make choices and fulfil their potential, we in turn are renewed and fulfilled. The 'doing something' has become a united 'being there' for each other.

Luke 6.18 also has Jesus himself proclaiming this good news of reciprocity:

Give and it will be given to you –
A good measure,
pressed down, shaken together,
running over,
will fall into your lap.
For whatever measure you give out
will be the measure you get back.

The final word in this chapter must be about a new project, started in September 1999, at St James. The minister, Janet Lees, is a speech therapist as well as an ordained minister, and has arranged with the new initiative, Sure Start, for a project for young children with speech and language delay, called 'Let's Talk'. More ministry for the needy through the front door, and blessing for the 'saints' by the back door!

# Aged

### – and Simeon who Waits to See Salvation

One of the indices of deprivation in most 'counts' in recent decades has been the number of residents over sixty or sixty-five. And old people are the poorest group, on any estimate, of people nationwide. In fact, the number of people in this age group is not excessively high in all our areas. There are various reasons for this. The male expectation of life is only sixty-eight years in Burngreave, as against seventy-six in Sheffield's western suburbs. The frequency of heart disease, cancer and work-related illness means that many men die before sixty-five.

There are other reasons why some old folk who belong here are not here any more. Crucial parts of our area have been crushed forever by the demolition of 2,500 homes in the 1970s. The quality of the homes which were destroyed can be seen in Grimesthorpe, where the accident of the inner ring road meant that the buildings were in a different planning area, so they were left standing – or forgotten? Otherwise, from Spital Hill to Burngreave Bank across to Owler Lane, everything was flattened. Fortunately, the little homes with twee garden spaces that replaced them in the 1980s were an improvement on the blocks of maisonettes built in the 1960s, which survive on Verdon Street and Woodside. But the people had been dispersed. Many of the vital pieces of human connectedness, which sustain a community, were destroyed. Gone was the traditional working-class situation, in which a grandmother – the local name is Nan Nan – continues to care for her sons or daughters and their sons and daughters, probably in the same street. Single parents could be accommodated in such a system, of course. Now, old people, single or couples, live one or two

expensive bus rides away from their offspring and their offspring's offspring. The good ones maintain a weekly visit.
Others keep in touch irregularly, or on birthdays. Many old
people do not have telephones, and live isolated lives. Thus,
when The Furnival seeks out people on their own on Christmas
Day, it has been isolated single old men whom they have
persuaded to come out from behind their sometimes boarded
up (for safety) maisonettes and to join us for a free Christmas
dinner.

Older people are tremendous resources in our areas. Some of
our older members remained behind, when all their relatives
had left, as witnesses and prophets, as signs of continuity and
wholesomeness in the midst of what to others was cataclysmic
change. Like Simeon in Luke 2. 29–32, they had looked for the
consolation of Israel, and now find themselves saying:

> Master, now you can let your servant go in peace,
> According to your word,
> For my eyes have witnessed your salvation
> Prepared for all the nations.
> A light for revelation to those outside
> And glory for your faithful inside.

We often comment that our old people's lunch clubs are run
by people in their eighties for people in their sixties! The eighty-
year olds are mainly the long-standing church members – the
'old faithfuls'. It has never occurred to them that they would do
any other than support their church, and do what they could to
service its operations. There is local authority money to provide
old people with cooked meals, and our brilliant community
transport minibuses to bring them, and a few younger people to
be drivers and escorts. So, of course, it is the task of those who
have spent their lives looking after others to do the work in the
kitchens or in the lunchrooms. 'What else would I be doing?'
they reply when asked about their persistence and courage,
often in the face of their own sickness or declining health. Or
perhaps they will say, 'Well, it keeps me out of mischief.'

In 1995, when St James URC had its major refit and moderni-
zation, many outside SICEM questioned the endeavour. 'Why
do all this for a few old people?' they asked. Barry Swift, a
member of St James, who was URC District Secretary, quickly
assured them that it was not entirely true that they were 'a few
old people', but also that there was a dual purpose in the
scheme – to utilize spare land for priority housing, and to make
funds available to equip the building for local community use as
well as for the members. But the abiding contemporary story of
St James has to be the amazing commitment of the five elderly
ladies who until 1998 provided the Tuesday Lunch Club.
It must have been the only lunch club run by people in their
eighties mainly for people in their thirties and forties. 'Thank
you so much for coming,' they said to the students who came
over from UTU for the immaculately prepared soup, jacket
potatoes, toasted sandwiches and home-made pies and cakes.

One of the saints of SICEM was Florrie Harrold. Florrie was
born in 1904. Her childhood and much of her married life
were lived in Colver's Yard, a collection of tiny cottages with
outside toilets, built into the hillside in Grimesthorpe. Her
life, remembered lovingly by so many, was a rich, eccentric,
generous web of busy doings: countless trips and events
organized by Florrie for all who wanted to come, to seaside or
local woods; nursing the sick, visiting everybody possible,
scouring markets for 'pots' and much else to sell on her stalls at
church bazaars; organizing shelter from bombing raids; enlist-
ing help from anyone she met for her endless projects; giving
everybody something – a sweet or a scone or anything of hers
they admired. Her whole life was an extension of 'chapel',
dressing folk up for fancy dress events, concert parties or Whit
processions, endlessly raising money with her jumble sales or
white elephant stalls, or visiting, caring for everyone in sight,
holding court in her open house on her birthdays.

In her last years, her body barely carried all her activity,
though she 'battled on'. She had osteoporosis and was bent
double, with twisted spine and swollen legs, so that you had
to stoop right down to look into her eyes – lively, sparkling,

trusting – and hear her voice – small, indomitable, cheerful, optimistic, encouraging. A striking and typical story was when she was burgled in August 1991. Jenny Hales tells the tale in the book she wrote about Florrie entitled, *It Were Lovely*, which Grimesthorpe Methodist Church published in 1992.

Florrie had begun to sleep in her living room, and often left the light on at night. It was an effort to go and lock her front door, then the back one, and anyway, she trusted everyone! She spent the nights sleeping a little between bouts of pain that woke her up and had her tottering from bed to chair, from chair to bed. Into this, about 3 am, burst a tall young man demanding money. She explained there was only £3 in her purse. He took it. He then picked up the Mission Box. 'You can't have that!', she said 'It's for the chapel!' He put it down again!

'Why don't you make yourself a cup of tea? You're a nice looking lad, you could do a lot better for yourself than this! Have you got a grandmother? No? That explains a lot, then, why you haven't been better brought up!' She told us later: 'I'm not upset, just sad for youngsters today. I forgive him.' She had a lot to forgive him, because he then took from her finger her late husband Reuben's ring. 'Don't do that,' she said, 'Reuben put that there sixty years ago.'[1]

When Gary, the thief, read the story in the *The Star*, he was so ashamed that he posted the ring back to the police, writing, 'I am really sorry. I didn't realize what I was doing. I was drunk, and hope I can be forgiven.' Florrie reported this back to us at chapel. 'It is really good news, isn't it?' she said. Florrie's only problem was that Gary was caught. She wrote to the police to try to get him off. When he got four years in jail, she was devastated, and wrote regularly to him, which Jenny continued to do. On one occasion, Gary wrote to Jenny: 'Things are not as bad as they seem. Florrie made me realize a lot of things. No matter how you feel, or what you do, what you have been through, all the ups and downs we may suffer, there is always someone who cares. She was one of those people, ready to help.' Jenny carried on writing to Gary.

> Why do I write to Gary? Why do I visit him? Because he was Florrie's friend. (Florrie's friend? – I thought he was her burglar!) That was just it! Every encounter with another human being, and whoever you were, whether you wished her good or ill or neither, she was your friend. Instant friend.

Incidentally, we need a book about Jenny Hales who, at seventy-five, is still herself continuing and expanding in her own ways the Florrie Harrold tradition on the streets of Grimesthorpe.

Time would fail to tell of all the saints around SICEM. But as a pure historical fact, I must record that there would be no SICEM but for – at certain stages – the four with average age of seventy at Lopham Street, and the five with average age of seventy-five (my mother, now a hundred and nine, rather pushed the average up!) at Grimesthorpe. So, 'old men/women dreaming dreams' (Acts 2. 17) is one of the seeds of new life in the city. And one of the priceless elements that, whatever the tragedies and traumas, helps hold it all together.

# 14

# Consumers

## – and the Seeds of Change Growing Secretly

Inner city areas often have appalling levels of ill-health. Apart from the absence of many of the health facilities available elsewhere, the ill-health is often the result of bad diet – crisps, sliced bread, chips, processed foods, tinned food, fatty food and very little fruit and vegetables.

For three years, 1977–79, we organized Pulse Wholefoods Store, run by volunteers on Spital Hill, in our area. Now, in 2000, we are opening a new larger project in the Spital Hill shopping area. Already, the New Roots shop, in the Broomhall inner city area, opposite the university, is part of the Ashram Centre. It is a project which helps people to eat better. It also helps poor people to eat better, by giving a 10% discount to unemployed, pensioners and students.

What do they think they are doing? It is about levelling, justice, sustainability. It is like the Kingdom of God which Jesus in Mark 4. 26–29 compares to the seed growing secretly.

Jesus also said:
'The Kingdom of God is as if
Someone scatters seed on the ground,
And they go to bed and get up night and day.

And the seed grows up and matures –
they do not know how.

The earth produces from within itself –
first the shoot, then the head,
then the grain in the head.

Then when the grain is ripe,
they go in with the sickle
because it's harvest time.'

Scattering seed on the ground has a two-fold meaning for the
New Roots shop.

First, it is about the shop as a place of sowing the seeds of
serious questions about radical change, seeds of new attitudes,
of caring about non-exploitative living. The seeds are the seeds
of total lifestyle change. The Gospel word for this is metanoia,
inadequately translated as 'repentance', but properly translated
as 'conversion', if by conversion we mean a real re-orientation
to a new perspective, a wholesale 'about-turn'.

For just such a wholesale turn-about is what the students,
mothers and unemployed look for, who serve as volunteers in
the New Roots shop. They are all deeply concerned about the
exploitation of the world and of people all around us, which
manifests itself in Meadowhall, in Supermarkets, in the IMF,
the Gatt Agreements on world trade, the slowness to relieve
poor countries of debt.

What can be done about all this? Well, start the seeds of a
revolution in attitudes. Begin it at the bottom. Begin it with
students, a new generation who will in the future be making
more important decisions. Begin it with some tangible gestures,
some acted parable, some miniature of a better state of things
and a better way of doing things. Sow a seed of radical change
now, that will in the future issue in a great harvest!

The second resonance for the New Roots shop of the seed
growing secretly is in the action of the seed as a model of ecology and sustainability. The seed grows and matures from within itself, within the dark of the earth. The miracles of the shoot,
the head and the grain all occur without human intervention –
while the sower 'goes to bed and gets up, night and day'. The
sower really is not the significant person. All s/he had to do was
to let the wondrous little power source, the seed, be placed
within the womb of its mother, the earth.

New Roots shop tries to be an ethical shop, an ecological

shop, a shop where the new future for all creation is manifested in parabolic form, in the physical form of real things which you can buy and eat. It is a place where the two concerns about ecology and justice are woven together, concerns which often run parallel with separate devotees. Here they are seen as a whole, in the struggle for 'fair' not 'free' trade. A current New Roots leaflet explains how it all works:

We are running a shop which is 'different'.
* We sell fruit and veg, wholefoods, snacks, Traidcraft, cards, local crafts – a rich and interesting variety.
* Our purpose is not to make money but to highlight a whole variety of issues.
* Our concerns are raised by the products we sell, and involve wider issues of justice and peace.
* We support people trying to make changes in their life-styles.
* The shop is run entirely by volunteers. We make decisions collectively.
* We aim to sell goods that:
– exploit neither people nor planet
– encourage awareness of the ethical issues underlying shopping
– are reasonably priced
– offer an alternative to mainline shops
* We use the shop window as a campaign display area, producing displays ourselves and inviting other groups to do so. There is also display space inside the shop.
* We are non-profit making.

New Roots opened in 1987. To celebrate its first ten years, Grace Vincent, its honorary co-ordinator, wrote a booklet on it called *New Roots: Shop for Justice*. In the last chapter, she summarizes what is for her and the other volunteers the 'Good News from a Shop'. She names ten 'aspects of a radical faith' visible in the shop:

   1. Returning to the Street. Churches meet behind closed

doors, in buildings others don't enter, as if meeting secretly. A shop is a common thoroughfare, where people easily walk in, where they do their business. Christianity began in the public places of Galilee at the street level.

2. Raising the Significance of Everyday Things. We deal in tomatoes, lentils, bread; basic elements of common human survival – things which are life-sustaining, pleasure-giving, symbols of richness and fruitfulness.

3. Acting Justly. People trust us to be honest and fair, to tell the truth about our products, to make only modest profit.

4. Standing for Something. We are seen as people with convictions and principles, clearly running a business for reasons other than profit, and trying to act on our beliefs.

5. Believing in the Power of Quite Simple Choices. New Roots is based on the premise that consumers have the capacity to affect whole industries. We have 'boycotts' of offending products – and 'buycotts' of fairtrade ones.

6. Declaring Our Interdependence as Human Beings. There is a new awareness, a slow change in the attitudes of millions of people that our action, our buying, is not neutral but has economic and political consequences for others.

7. Deliberately Creating Oddity and Provocative Juxtaposition. A Bible and a cross in the window above the apples, nectarines, and leeks, or a model of the cardboard shelter of the homeless beside the lentils and beans, compel thought, and provide 'bridges' or at least uncomfortable provocations between simple acts of buying and vast global issues.

8. Exposing the Hidden Connection. Who would know that a harmless tin of baked beans comes to us from a company that pollutes the environment and is linked with the arms trade?

9. Acknowledging the Complexities. Many of the issues are much more complex than buying coffee from poor people rather than rich multinationals. Should we buy produce from the other side of the world? Or flowers from Colombia, knowing how the workers suffer from pesticides?

10. Asserting That All Things Hold Together. Our good

news is somehow about humanity and ecology, mutuality and tolerance, about how everything 'holds together'.[1]

Ashram Community Trust is a small national and ecumenical Christian radical community.[2] The Trust bought 347 Glossop Road in 1987. There are three sections to the project. Upstairs is a flat for people involved in the work. In the basement is the Ashram Centre room. Most important is the New Roots Shop. The Ashram Community Trust, a registered charity, allows the New Roots shop, consisting of ACT members and others, to carry on their business, because it is coherent with the Trust's charitable aims, and because it is not for individual profit or payment to volunteers or workers. The New Roots shop is not itself a charity, and its finances are separate from those of ACT. Chris Bullock and Grace Vincent are the long-time Ashram volunteers, plus many others.

Ashram Community also runs two Ashram Community Houses on our side of the city, at 75 and 77 Rock Street in the Pye Bank/Woodside area, near to The Furnival. Two volunteer workers in New Roots, Marcus Scott and Helen Platt, moved into No. 75 in October 1996. With Peter Hurley, the other resident, they developed 'An Ecological Rule of Life'. Marcus wrote:

> The motivation to live ecologically stems, I think, from two main sources. The first is realizing the impact we have on the environment around us and trying to reduce this. A scientific consensus is now agreed on what are the most serious problems affecting the world: global warming, ozone depletion, acid rain, toxic pollution, species extinction, deforestation, land degradation, water depletion and non-renewable resource depletion. In addition, however, ecological living is about living equitably as a global citizen; not taking more than a fair share. The figures are quite well publicized, with a fifth of the world population using up three quarters of the world resources, the classic division between 'north' and 'south'.

The following describes some of the basic measures which the three House members at Rock Street implemented to get their house into ecological order. Marcus again:

*Food*    Marcus and Helen are vegans whilst Peter is a vegetarian. If 'Northern' consumption levels are taken seriously, a 70% reduction would be required to create a fairer distribution. In terms of food, meat and dairy products are the most obvious to reduce or cut out because they are a very inefficient way of getting protein. In addition, for us, there is the issue of how animals are treated, particularly dairy herds.

In the garden at Rock Street, I try to grow some vegetables and I am part of a collective that works some allotments. Conventional farming requires large inputs of energy and ultimately degrades the wider environment. Growing some of your own vegetables ensures they are organic, makes efficient use of land and means that transport, pollution and packaging are not necessary. We do not grow anywhere near as much as we consume, and we are lucky enough to be able to have a weekly delivery of a box of organic produce.

*Transport*    Apart from my studying part-time at Leeds, we all live close to where we work and to an extent that was a conscious decision. We all use public transport and I ride a bike. Peter recently acquired a car for his job as RC Deanery Youth Worker, although this has been a point of contention in the house!

*Water*    We have a flushing policy for the toilet, so the clean, fresh, drinkable water used for this function is kept to a minimum. There has been the idea of having a compost toilet outside in the shed, but this is a long term plan. We have water butts outside connected to both the roof guttering and the bathroom sink.

*Recycling*    We are part of a local recycling run which makes the practice feasible. To use an individual car to take materials to be recycled, for example, results in damage to the environment which outweighs the benefits from the recycling itself.

How significant are all these aspects of an 'ecological rule of life'? Change has to start somewhere, and to start in small ways. Marcus comments:

> Attempting to live more ecologically does not mean going without, but it does mean altering some basic elements of an average 'industrial life style' which centres around a meat-based diet and the use of the car. We believe, at Rock Street, that in our daily living, in a small way, we have a chance to affect the awful division of resources in the world and the environmental 'ecocide' we are fast approaching. We are not doing very much, and the changes we have made are small, but they have become habit. It is an ongoing process and there is continually room for improvement.

But it is a seed of change, hopefully for the future world. And it is a seed already growing among us, in our earth.

In fact, in Autumn 1998, Helen and then Peter separately moved out of 75 Rock Street and into council rented flats in Verdon Street, thus embodying The Furnival community's solidarity with its neighbourhood. So our prime aim for the Community House had been fulfilled! Meantime, our attempts to set up a local 'Burngreave Hands-On' Volunteer Service based at 77 Rock Street were frustrated by the government ending the whole Opportunities for Volunteering scheme.

So, in 2000, we in the Sheffield Ashram Branch are looking for ways to develop a project/house/agency in the Burngreave area which will continue and expand the ecology/healthy living/new roots/self-development agendas. We will continue our two Community Houses at 75 and 77 Rock Street. But we now have a new base, more suited to these developments. Watch this space! Decisions are being made, as this book is being published, about the Burngreave Ashram at 86 Spital Hill, which comprises a shop and basement for a New Roots-style outlet, a three-bedroomed community flat, a large community room, and extensive works and workshop area.[3]

Inderjit Bhogal says that the 'triple jeopardy' of the inner

cities is 'Many poor, many religions, and many trees'. He pro-
claims:

> We live in a world of many poor, but also of many religions,
> many skin colours, and a world of many trees (still). We are
> women and men, of different abilities. Poverty, plurality,
> pollution and environmental issues, racism and sexism are all
> central concerns. All are crying out for life and love, for bread
> and beauty.[4]

Poverty, faith and ecology are inter-related. Can the brown
field sites of the post-war industrial cities be pioneer locations
for consumers becoming gardeners, exploiters becoming libera-
tors, and victims of the human rape of the earth becoming co-
operators in the 'work for the new community of all creation',
as a phrase in the Ashram Community's Membership Commitment has it?

# PART THREE

# DRINKING FROM OUR OWN WELLS

*Spiritualities and Strategies for Christians and Churches*

*Into earth's unfolding story*
*Breaks the sign of timelessness;*
*Hidden yet revealed the glory*
*Of eternal hopefulness;*
*Through our history of tears,*
*Jesus leads us through our fears.*
*Men and women, stop all grieving,*
*Though these times are filled with pain;*
*For the poor start believing*
*That all life can rise again;*
*Rise to mercy, truth and peace,*
*Bring to victims just release.*
*Others gain through our believing,*
*Catch our hope and share our faith;*
*Find new strength when we are singing*
*Of our God with human face.*
*Sing of loving strong and sure,*
*Sing out loudly for the poor.*
*His the song and his the struggle,*
*He the joy which spurs us on;*
*His the grace which does enable*
*Faithfulness to overcome*
*Sleepless nights and doubting days*
*With the timelessness of praise*

Clive Scott

# 15

# Telling it the Way it Is

## – and Jesus' Retreat with his Disciples

Constantly coming and going and hardly having time to share all the things we have been doing and teaching, we try to get times of retreat. Sometimes it is a Team Ministry Day, sometimes the SICEM July Half Day, sometimes a meeting of the Community Work Committee or the SICEM Council Open Meeting. Often it is our Sunday worship occasions which, as Ian Lucraft says, provide us with three vital things:

1. A desire for space to recharge batteries that are run down in the disproportionate amount of church related community work, done by such a small number of people.

2. A space to be open about our real ambitions for change in the world, which are subsumed in our daily work, and unintelligible to others in the mainstream structures some work in.

3. A chance to be hugged, metaphorically, by a loving community who want you to be part of them.

Whenever it is, and wherever, we find ways of sharing, of telling each other our stories, of recounting the bits of tragedy and triumph on our streets. Like Jesus' first disciples, we have been out 'on mission', and need to come back together to share all the things we have been doing and teaching – as it was for the first disciples in Mark 6. 30–31:

The ones who had been sent out by Jesus gathered around him and started telling him all the things that they had been doing and teaching.

Jesus responded: 'Let us go off, just by ourselves, to some deserted place where we can rest for a while.' For there were so many other people coming and going, that they could not even get time to have some food. So they set off together, just by themselves, in a boat, and found a deserted place.

There, unfortunately, they did not, at least at first, have time to share. There is, in fact, no record of what the first disciples reported to Jesus on the occasion in Mark 6. We know the record says they had gone out to preach that people should change themselves, and to cast out demons and anoint the sick (Mark 6. 12–13). Their message was presumably the one which Jesus declared at the beginning. There is no other preaching message of Jesus or the disciples in Mark, apart from the clear and simple one of Mark 1.15:

> The Kairos has arrived.
> The Realm of God is right here.
> Change yourselves completely.
> And trust yourselves to the Good News.

This easily remembered message is presumably what had to be received and the messenger welcomed (Mark 6.10) or 'received and heard' (v. 11). Luke says they preached 'the Kingdom of God', and Matthew 'the Kingdom of heaven is at hand'. Apart from the crowds who come to Jesus, we do not know whether the disciples' preaching led to many people understanding what was going on. As for healing, we know from elsewhere that the disciples, though asked to heal a spirit-possessed boy, were unable to do so (Mark 9. 14–18). They criticized others who used the name of Jesus for healing (Mark 9. 38–41), but do not seem to have been so good at it themselves. Indeed, Jesus often chides them for not doing the right thing, or not understanding (e.g. Mark 7.18). So, what did they have to say, when they poured out – or wanted to – all the things they had been doing and teaching? We do not know. Perhaps it was very much a mixture of failures and successes, disappointments and encouragements. At any rate, it has always been with us.

I noted down the things we shared at one of our SICEM July Half Days.

At St James, Duncan Wilson reported on former members coming back – 'returnees', like Astrid Gillespie. And there was the continuing parable of the Tuesday Lunch Club and the multi-cultural, multi-ethnic, multi-racial Sunday worship.

At Pitsmoor, there had been a sudden influx of sixteen girls into the flagging Girls Brigade – 'Miracles do happen', said Janice Gear. The Monday Lunch Club story of Jan Royan and Iain Cloke was of a one-to-one club for local people with learning difficulties. John and Pam Eaton told of the impossible situation of repeated vandalism in the Youth Club carried out by a particular family, and how they still held to a 'No bars here' policy.

Lopham Street saw its task , said Duncan Wilson, as 'to provide a home for other people who can do Gospel things we cannot do', such as the Nomad voluntary organization to help homeless people get homes and furniture, or the Teenage Black Mums and Toddlers Group, or the Old People's Lunch Club.

Shiregreen, said Gwen Smithies, had been 'sacking Sunday School staff', with eight of the congregation now 'taking the kids in turns'. They hoped to develop their work with local kids – which later led to a part-time Shiregreen Project for Gwen with children and families. Also, said Peter Smithies, there was the ongoing miracle of the way money came together for replacing the two SICEM minibuses of Pitsmoor and Shiregreen Community Transport. A Sponsored Hymnsing had brought in £500.

At the Ashram Centre/New Roots Shop near the university, it was the story of 'a church to evangelize the ecologists'. We gathered people in a post-church ecological Christianity, in which young people and students allied themselves to a movement for change, rather than to a credal worship, said Richard Griffiths – though there was Tuesday evening worship, too.

At Upper Wincobank, on the Flower Estate, it was stories of 'Walking the Good News' – Geoff King walking their dog, loitering with intent; of 'Catering the Good News' – Kate King, catering for parties and needy kids;[1] and of 'The Non-

Generation Gap' – Gill Lemm telling how the church has joined the Sunday School rather than the other way round.

At Grimesthorpe, it was the story of discovering the value of worship in the front shop room, much to the surprise of the oldest members, Florrie Harrold and Florrie Greaves. The experience of living in the flat and the pain and tragedy of trying to help the local young people, was told by Chris Pritchard. And there was Jenny Hales, settling in as 'Church rep' on the streets, after moving from the West of the City to the East End as a volunteer missioner.

In the Eucharist Congregation, it was the continuing life of an occasion extra to denominational church life, 'Something Different', which Chris Bullock reported. Grace Vincent said it was also about Projects started and groups formed which developed and went their own ways, such as Liberation Congregation, Ashram Centre/New Roots, Pitsmoor Youth Housing Trust. And it was about a model that people take away, and use to create their own indigenous congregations, on the lines of Alternative Church.[2]

The heart of the Urban Theology Unit, said Iain Cloke, continued to be above all 'the UTU process', vocational discernment. It was also the use of the inner city and the SICEM projects as seed-beds for people to come and discover their own vocations.

When we had shared our stories, we had a time of open reflection. The twenty-five of us present discussed the significance of the stories we had heard. Immediately, we observed that there were stories with common elements, which seemed to us to be significant for Christian reasons – because they had coherence in some way with Gospel elements. So we began to build up a check list of 'characteristics' – characteristics of the Gospel and characteristics of our current experiences. I wrote down furiously!

1. Risk-taking. The stories are about being prepared to be risk-takers, taking risks about people, taking risks with yourself, taking risks with our churches. Faith-acting is essentially risk-taking – doing something which will only be proved 'right'

later, and then only if it coheres with some part of the ongoing Jesus-action.

2. Failure as positive. There is a refusal to regard failure as failure. In fact, all the stories are positive. All the failures are glossed over, as not very significant, as not the vital thing. In fact, we realized that we could have told innumerable stories about disasters, disappointments, betrayals or 'flops'. But we find that we move on, accepting the failure and going on to do other things – making a stumbling block into a stepping stone. Dwelling on disasters does not help.

3. Persistence and faith. We persisted with things that would have been written off elsewhere, that produce no good results. You slog on and slog on for the little bit that might rub off. It is a story of faith, holding on to 'faith' that the Girls' Brigade is important, or that youngsters might change, or that buyers of muesli might see the point of the shop.

4. Individual initiative. People start up and use what they have, responding to situations, not sitting down and strategizing. We don't question each other when someone says, 'Why can't we do so-and-so?' We say, 'Go ahead. We'll support you.' Whether you are thinking of the little core groups of Christians, or of those whose lives are touched, it's people on the edges of life, hanging on, but taking their lives into their hands at times.

5. Love-hate relationships. Very difficult and deprived young people are a real burden. We painfully learn to 'Love one another as I have loved you' (John 15. 12) – an unlimited love, done to us, which we do to others as an ongoing thing.

6. Sowing seed. Often you do not see what seeds might come to fruition later. Sometimes you do see it. But other seeds that you may never know about could produce something somewhere else. We see things 'rubbing off' on people. We see people changing – and ourselves changing.

7. Success. We observed that no one had mentioned success, except to decry it. The goal is not success. It is something else which is motivational. Often, we are making progress by standing still. Some people cannot do this but are always seeking to

prove what they have achieved. This is not our method. Anyway, if you had succeeded, you would stop, and it would all be over! The fact that we are still here is the 'success', that we have stories to tell at all!

8. Jesus stories. The stories of Jesus are in the background. The Jesus actions function as a repeated model or dynamic. We don't have to produce texts all the time, but it is a determining thing, telling us what is important, and giving us the instincts and the imagination to do certain things, and not to do other things.

9. Story-acting. We do the story as a way of telling it. It's a re-enacting of the story of Jesus in our stories. We do not have to tell a good story, we are acting a good story. When we do talk, it's simply to describe what has been happening. We have moved from being story-hearers to being story-actors and thus story-creators.

10. Worship. We noticed that no one had told stories of our worship. This was not because it was unimportant. But our worship and fellowship life arise out of and are supportive and inspirational for our faith and action, which are primary. We use UTU's *Hymns of the City*,[3] and other material. But mostly we produce worship spontaneously, extempore, in an open, participatory way, welcoming the contributions of everyone present, and not usually with endless new pieces of paper!

Such were the notes I took on that July day. From them, a few sermons were preached, as we took the stories round the little churches, and invited others into the conversation. So we 'gathered round Jesus' and continued 'telling him all the things we had been doing and teaching'. Interestingly, on this occasion there was more reference to general Gospel notes than to specific Gospel stories as the model for what had been happening. And there were strong implicit theological discernments going on, as I have observed.

Later, Duncan Wilson tackled this over a period in a talk he gave – and developed – at UTU. He called it 'Gospel Values in Inner City Churches'. It's in *Gospel from the City*. The list in fact arises out of a long description of SICEM's congregations and their life. Some of the characteristics are like the ones just named. His full list goes as follows.

> Our grasp and expression of 'Gospel Values' in the Inner City Church . . . is . . .
> Where Christ and his people are,
> they make clear that everyone is a child of God;
> > that those not within the church are not necessarily far from the Kingdom of God;
> they lay a table where all are welcome, where strangers find a home;
> they recognize that everyone has an offering to bring;
> they find faith where no one else looks for it;
> they notice people whom others ignore or diminish;
> they celebrate the 'greatness of the small';
> they give space for everyone to fail, to learn, to grow;
> they make mercy and generosity servants of renewal;
> they never force an entry into other people's lives;
> they warn against making rules more important than relationships;
> they show that love finds joy in being spent;
> > that being broken or vulnerable also reveals God's presence;
> they expect change to be possible for everyone;
> they patiently wait to find each person's 'touching place';
> > and promise that, wherever Christ is,
> > > the blind do recover their sight,
> > > the lame do walk,
> > > the deaf do hear,
> > > the dumb do speak,
> > > the dying are brought to life
> > > and the poor do hear good news.[4]

The ethos becomes part of our inheritance! Duncan's successor, Janet Lees, stated her 'Words of Recommitment' thus, at her Induction in September 1998:

I recommit myself to the Holy One,
To the company of Christ's friends
And the highway of the Spirit of Wisdom.

I concur with the gospel call to repentance,
looking inside myself and round about
for those things which impede
God's commonwealth of justice and peace.

I embrace life on the margins of church and society,
a sentinel, fully sentient,
hunting for and gathering together
gifts of use in the building of community.

# 16

# Twos and Threes

## – and Peter and James and John

I've heard it said in Preachers' Meetings occasionally. But not, happily, in SICEM. 'There'll only be two or three there – it's not worth having a service for just that number. It's not worth the preacher going to conduct worship for only two or three.' The 'only two or three' is a classic put down for the small congregation.

Of the twelve whom Jesus chose 'as his companions, so that they might be with him' (Mark 3.14), the two or three – Peter, James and John – seem to have formed an 'inner core' of people who were nearest to him. Indeed, Jesus takes only them with him on certain decisive occasions, like the 'transfiguration'. So Mark 9.2:

> Six days later
> Jesus took Peter and James and John
> And brought them with him to a high mountain
> Alone, just by themselves.

It's very like our little churches. Except that at Grimesthorpe, our three were nearly always women. At one time, a few years ago, there were just four active members in the membership. There was Florrie Harrold, the incredible old lady whose story we told in chapter 13. The other three members were Jenny Hales, who at sixty-five decided to move from Broomhill on the prosperous west of Sheffield, to come and live and work in Grimesthorpe; Louise Gough, who came from Southlands College to test her vocation to Christian ministry, and lived in the flat above the shop through a period of hard self-discovery;

and Grace, my wife, who had moved to Grimesthorpe in the early 1970s to help keep it going. My mother, confined to our home, was an absent member also.

One recalls how, after all the disciples had forsaken him and fled, the three named women took over the disciples' duties of care and standing-by during the passion and crucifixion, the burial and the resurrection – Mary Magdalene, Mary the Mother of James, and Salome (Mark 16.1).

What did it mean that Jesus took only the three with him up the Mount of Transfiguration? That it is the three who are leaders-in-waiting, James and John and Peter? That they alone go to the Garden of Gethsemane with him (Mark 14.33)? That three women care for his body? And that he himself says, 'Where two or three are gathered together in my name, it is I myself who is present with them' (Matt. 18.20)?

Two or three, or four, is the number of a group of friends. That number of mothers come round for a chat. That number of lads or girls go out together on the town. That number would be the number of 'mates of mine' in the local pub. For a Christian community to be that number seems to me to be natural and good. In the Gospel story, only the three know some of the secrets. I recall Dietrich Bonhoeffer's 'Arcane Discipline' – a secret discipline of discipleship shared only between a few close friends. I recall Karl Barth's 'difference' – not the 'difference' between those who are saved and those who are not saved, but the difference between those who know and those who do not know – and that probably those who 'know' are few.

We in the churches have become accustomed to larger numbers. The original words of the third verse of Edward Perronet's hymn, 'All hail the power of Jesus' name' are apparently not the ones we sing today:

> You seed of Israel's chosen race
> You ransomed from the fall

But rather the much more controversial but evocative:

You seed of Israel's chosen race
A remnant weak and small

So, at any rate, the current *Baptist Praise and Worship* has it.

In March 1996, we were down to four faithful members at Lopham Street: Mary Pilgrim, her brother, Jack Simmerson, and Anne and Frank Digby. For three or four years, they had been worshipping fortnightly in each others' homes. Their cars got vandalized if they went down to the old chapel on Sunday evenings. Then, at the Circuit Meeting on 6 March it was decided that the old chapel at Lopham Street was finally to be closed on Palm Sunday. Two weeks before, I had found a public house for sale, only 150 yards from the chapel. Suddenly everyone had said: 'This is it!' We had to go out in faith and go to the auction and I made our bid for £49,500 which was £32,500 more than we had from selling Lopham Street!

The Minister, Duncan Wilson, then told of Jane Grinonneau's visit two days before, and of her sense of call to be part of it. Jane was a Baptist Minister from Northfield, Birmingham, who had been looking for a place to minister among people. She walked round the area and caught a vision of a ministry there, which would use her skills as nurse, teacher and worker with families and children. Lopham Street had welcomed this and asked her to be the local pastor. Jane had agreed to come, without salary at that stage. Duncan added: 'At Lopham Street, the faithfulness of the four all through the dark days has been incredible. They just stood firm, and kept on when everything seemed against them. But now, we seem to be going with the flow.'

We didn't know what word to use. I asked in the Circuit Meeting for a scripture that described what one felt like when things just kept on happening, unplanned but 'right'. Amy Richinson said, 'It's the sense of awe' in Acts 2. 43. She was right. We all felt a sense of awe, that things were happening, that we could not plan them, that something awesome was taking place. We were going with ' what God was doing', going with 'Gospel things happening', going with 'the dynamic of the movement of Jesus', going with the 'faithfulness' of Lopham Street, going with the 'call' of Jane and then others after her. It was as if, once the mad decision had been made, Gospel madness catches on – as in Acts 2.43, where the 'sense of awe' among the early Christians comes in the midst of faithful devotion, having things in common, people bringing gifts, and 'signs and wonders'.

And so it continued. Ashram Community had a community house just up the hill in Andover Street for ten years (1971–81), and had recently decided that it should re-establish a community house somewhere in the area. The Furnival opportunity meant it was clear what was needed. Not a project (The Furnival has plenty of room for projects), but a small house nearby where we could have some people living who would help the work on the ground. So Ashram Community was buying a house in Rock Street. Into this came Peter Hurley, a Roman Catholic who had left seminary because he wanted to work more alongside people in a poor area. The previous August, he had been staying at the local Catholic Presbytery, and had visited around Verdon Street, and had said to himself: 'This is the kind of place I want to be and find a way to minister.'

Once one thing happens, there are 'signs following'. As Clive Scott's hymn has it:

Others gain through our believing,
Catch our hope and share our faith.
Find new strength when we are singing
Of our God with human face.
Sing of loving strong and sure
Sing out loudly for the poor!

It was humbling to see how others came to help us. Other Sheffield circuits and churches made us gifts or loans. People out of the blue, as well as friends nearby, sent us money. What would we do? We did not know. We'd have a service each Sunday at 3 pm and we'd house our NCH Action for Children work and our old people's lunch club. Beyond that, we did not know.

A few base lines immediately emerged. First, we did not want to change it from looking like a pub. It was pleasant, light and homely inside. We had to do some major improvements to make a proper kitchen. But beyond that we wanted to leave it the same, so that people continued to feel at home in it. So we would keep the two bars and the fixed seating. Second, we wanted it to continue to be called The Furnival. As Jane said, even the word 'public house' is good. A 'public house of God' – a house of God for the general public, and not just the few. So we kept the old notice outside (painting out 'Tetley's'!). Third, we wanted to work with others in partnership, to develop meeting places and services, in which groups of local people could be involved, and some help be brought to a very needy area. So we looked around for allies. These were our first thoughts in winter 1996–97, when I was still officially involved. The 'we' has now become 'they'.

Meanwhile, at Grimesthorpe, Susannah and Jonathan Youdan arrived to study at UTU in September 1997, and chose to join Grimesthorpe, where Jonathan set about a local situation analysis. He found that in the 1991 Census dates, the enumeration districts around the chapel had a total population of 1297, divided as follows:

| Age | White | Pakistani | Black |
|---|---|---|---|
| 16–29 | 442 | 34 | 27 |
| 30–60/65 | 578 | 44 | 25 |
| Over 60/65 | 138 | 6 | 3 |

The total population of 25–29-year-olds was 262, with 185 children one to four years, and 131 children five to nine or 16% aged nine or under. This kind of fascinating detail was fed back to the church and indicated that, as against common perception, the area was not 'all old people' or 'mainly Asian'. A parents and toddlers group was the obvious next step, and a new understanding of the area. But, of course, it was Jonathan and Susannah, with their two small boys, who were the pioneers and workers for it. Situation analysis is essential, but it only works if there are people prepared to go where it leads.

Grimesthorpe in Autumn 1999 has thirteen members, a children's 'Jesus Club' and a Mums and Toddlers group, besides its old people's lunch club, several of whose members come to service now. The Furnival has had £250,000 of schemes and has eighteen members, open house and café weekday mornings, the Cellar Project for youth training, and numerous other enterprises, including being the base for Burngreave Credit Union.

But neither Grimesthorpe nor The Furnival would be there today had the twos and threes and fours not held on. And had those of us who stood by not also said: 'Leave it alone,' when everyone outside asked, 'When are you going to close it?' 'Leave it alone' was the cry of the gardener, you may recall, when the boss got tired of waiting for fruit from his fig tree, according to Jesus' parable in Luke 13. 6–9. 'Give me just one more year,' said the gardener. 'We might find some manure will work after all.' I have only two improvements to offer. One year may not be enough. And you never know in what shape the manure will come!

This, again, makes sense for us. Our experience is that these sayings are true, both in a personal sense and in a community sense. In a personal sense, we have seen so many people who did not need to be here, choose to come and 'lose themselves', or 'fall into the ground', or become incarnate, as we put it. They follow the model of Christ who 'emptied himself and took the form of a slave' (Phil. 2.7). Like Christ, they become subservient to the forces and powers at work in the area. And they usually 'come through', they become significant people: both fulfilled people and really useful people.

In a community sense, we have also seen this at work. Our little churches could be excused for seeking to save their own lives. At times, there are periods in which they do just that. But those times are only so that they can remain there, being on the ground, ready for a time when some new opportunity or some new people or some new state or council initiative appears, which needs them and their existence. Till that happens, they keep on telling the Gospel stories and keeping the Gospel community together.

The tiny numbers recall Jesus' images of the seed. If a single tiny mustard seed germinates and grows, a whole tree will result and that is what the Kingdom of God is like, he says (Luke 13. 20–21). That is what the future city is like, I say. The social services and planners and social theorists and administrators and councillors and MPs are desperate for some solid, dependable and proven pieces of life in the urban wilderness. They come and perch in our trees (v. 32!) if we stay long enough, make enough noise and produce at least some goods!

Another of Jesus' images is the woman taking only a little yeast, but it is enough to turn three measures of flour, to leaven a whole mix. That is what the Kingdom of God is like, he says (Luke 13. 20–21). This is what the future city is like, I say. You only need the tiny measure of yeast, and it will leaven the dough, and your loaf will rise, a loaf which is bread for all, bread for the world, bread for yourself and your neighbours. All the yeast has to do is to be prepared to give up its life for the sake of the bread which is to come, and be prepared, as we shall see, to be pummelled into shape, for the consumer's sake!

The seed has to disappear as seed. Jesus says, 'Unless a grain of corn falls into the ground, and dies, it remains on its own, just a single grain. But once it dies, it will bring forth much fruit' (John 12.24). Jesus said this of people who chose to regard their life as dispensable for the sake of others (v. 23). Or, as he says in Mark 8. 53, 'If you hold on to life, you will only lose it. But if you lose your life for my sake and the Gospel's sake you will actually keep it.' And, as Jesus in John 15.8 says, 'You will bring forth fruit, and so be my disciples.'

Three local stories belong here, of three singular people who 'did something'. Anita Day lived in Pye Bank. She went through the horrors of being made homeless, and started an informal network called Nomad that helped other homeless people. For a time they rented our basement at Lopham Street as a furniture store. Nomad is now a valuable Sheffield-wide organization. Grace Vincent was secretary of the Scott Road Neighbourhood Group and organized people to meet with planners. They discovered that a row of hoardings was to be built along Ellesmere Road. Grace said, 'Why not trees?' A hundred of them are there as her memorial! Ruth Crowley heard that Cable TV had permission to dig up the footpaths on upper Abbeyfield Road, which would have threatened the life of the beautiful old trees on the road. She organized a petition of all the residents and persuaded Cable TV to dig up the road instead.

Of course, the 'select few' or the 'surviving remnant' in a church are as open to the 'messiah syndrome' – the state of mind of someone ministering to others who thinks or acts as if they were 'the messiah' – as are social workers, community workers and ministers. People with 'messiah syndrome' are notoriously difficult to live with as colleagues, but also objectionable to clients because of their 'I'm doing good to you and it's good for you that I'm so special.' I confess that this is a danger. But it seems to me that what we need is some kind of 'messianic consciousness'. This phrase is used of Jesus – that he had a consciousness of being the chosen one, the anointed one, the messiah. It seems to me that some of the most significant and profound and fruitful people I have known could be described as having a messianic consciousness. That is, each of them has a sense of being someone significant, who is in some way 'called', or 'anointed', or 'set apart', to do or be something in relation to God's realm on earth and to the wholeness and salvation of humanity.

Only by speaking of such a consciousness, such a 'mind, as it was in Christ Jesus' (Phil. 2. 5), can I account for the sustaining, persistent commitment of people in often the most demanding and depressing situations, who yet act as if they were special and important people (which they are) doing special and important things, things which would simply disappear but for their deep sense of commitment to them, and their deep grounding in the mystery of God's love working in spite of everything. So long as there are twos and threes of people doing and acting 'messianically', there is hope for our cities and hope for our churches and hope for the ongoing saga of humanity.

# 17

# Incomers

## – and Jesus' Ministry of Incarnation

'Incomers' is a favourite word in the more stable of inner cities and housing estates – or indeed, in other areas of South Yorkshire. You can live in a place for many years and still be an 'incomer', or an 'offcomer', as some say. It is the opposite of 'local'.

'You'll always be an incomer – an outsider – you will never really belong here,' is sometimes said to those of us who feel the call to be part of inner cities and estates. Indeed, one of the sophistries of our middle-class detractors has through all my lifetime been the put-down of telling us, 'Oh well, of course you are not really the poor. The poor are those who cannot choose to be there. You can choose to be there. And you can always choose not to be there, which the true poor cannot.'

Recently, I have become less tolerant of this enlightened middle-class dismissal of those of us who are 'incomers' into areas of need. For a start, nobody could ever do anything for anybody, if they did not initially come into an area and try to tackle some of the problems. At the beginning, the problem often is the absence of people who can get a proper perspective on the local situation, sufficient to be able to see ways of development and change. And somebody has to do something if anything is going to change. The real contrast is not with people who come in, and those who are there already. The real contrast is between locals and incomers on the one side, and the permanent outsiders – those who presume to evaluate or dictate what is to be done, who never become incomers, but remain outsiders, be it as professionals or as critics.

Incidentally, it is also not true that 'You can always choose not to be there,' at least not if you have been mad enough to buy a house there. Grace and I recently realized that £10,000–£20,000 had been wiped off the value of our little inner city 1930s semi! We could not buy anything elsewhere, even if we wanted to!

Incomers can be useful, if they adopt an incarnational model of behaviour – and if they stay long enough. From a Christian point of view, the decisive model is incarnation, which certainly means being an 'incomer' – someone who comes in to share the life of the disadvantaged, to live alongside them, and then slowly to discover what ways they might work with those who are already there.

Indeed, I believe that the decisive gift of Christianity is this gift of incarnation – not just the gift of incarnation in Jesus, but the gift of constant incarnations. Each incarnation must begin from outside. It comes tentatively, fearfully to birth. It births itself in some part of the human milieu. It is subject to the disciplines, misunderstandings and oppressions of all around. It grows secretly, through silent years, growing till it is able furtively to appear. Then its 'messianic secret' suddenly comes out. An incarnation is a divine annunciation, a heavenly naming. And the Spirit demands a ludicrous claim that all people and all things and all communities will be changed – that the poor will get good news, the captives will get freedom, the broken will get wholeness (Luke 4.18).

Such is the heart of our theology. If it sounds odd or irrelevant, let me share three stories. The first is our experience with people coming to UTU and SICEM. For example at Grimesthorpe, since 1979, we have had a succession of outstanding single people living in the flat. The first residents were Margaret Mackley, Richard Levitt and Mark Woodhead. Later residents were Chris Sissons, Anne Lewis, Trish Stroud, Andy Cawthera, Ruth Thompson, John Tomlinson, Helen Bruce, Moira Neish, Tim Baker, Katrina Alton, Lynn Jolly, Richard Griffiths, Louise Gough, Judy Talbot, Francesca Signore, Neil Craig, Chris Pritchard, Elinor Wordsworth, Liz Jacobs and Karen Stapley. Each of them would say that their having been at Grimesthorpe for a period was a decisive part of discovering their vocational way.

Being an incomer, or being incarnate, has disciplines to it. Let me share two incidents from Jane Grinonneau's ministry at The Furnival. Both took place in May 1998.

One day, Jane was about to leave the area, when a local shop keeper ran from her shop to the adjacent phone box. Jane could hear her shout at the police down the phone 'Get here quick, he's in the post office.' Jane walked across to her. There was a man standing in the shop, shouting, plus some other customers, in much alarm.

'Do we know him?' Jane asked. 'Yes – it's Steve.' Jane went over to the post office. The door was locked. Several people were inside, frantic. Clearly Steve had been shop-lifting again. The squad car arrived. Jane spoke to the officer and said that Steve needed help. He was imprisoned by his heroin habit. 'I'm not going in,' the policeman said, 'I'm waiting for back-up.' It came – another police car, and the police helicopter overhead.

Jane was let into the post office. Steve just looked at her. 'Oh Jane,' he said. She put her arm round him, the tall black figure with yellowed eyes. The police came in and were gentle but firm, and handcuffs were applied. The local people in the post office said angrily to Jane, 'We are trying to make a difference round here.' Jane wondered, 'What am I supposed to be doing here?'

The second story is about an incident which took place a few weeks later.

One Sunday, Jane and her friends were preparing for worship in the lounge 'sanctuary'. Suddenly she realized that the master set of keys had been placed for a moment on the bar, and had been taken. No one was around, so someone must have run in and run off with them, perhaps mistaking them for car keys.

In the service, the sermon was on 'What does the Lord require of you?' in Micah 6.8:

Act justly,
Love mercy
Walk humbly with your God.

After worship, they all began to look for the keys. They could not believe they were not there. The day wore on and it became very dark. Then the vigil began. Jane and her husband David kept vigil in The Furnival all night. When it was clear that the keys were not going to reappear, at 3 am, Jane called a 24-hour locksmith who put new temporary padlocks all round the building. 'What is happening here?' the locksmith asked. Jane told him. He said, 'As it's you, and as it's this place, I'll only charge you £50.'

Jane returned home to try to get some sleep. At 9 am Jane was woken by a local woman saying, 'Can you take me to the market? I need some vegetables.' She did not know Jane had been up for most of the night. Later, walking round the premises, distressed and very tired, Jane had one of the local teenagers come and say she'd keep an eye out for the keys. An hour later, the teenager said she would get the keys, as she had seen them with some kids. 'The kids want some money from me. Will you give me some money?'

Jane said, 'Bring the keys, and you'll get some money.' But the teenager came back twice to say she could not find the kids. Finally, she just asked for some money. Jane, absolutely in bits, up all night, is asked for thirty pieces of silver! Two days later, every lock in the building – nine on the ground floor, one on the first floor, ten in the basement, were replaced. The bill was £600. Where are they to find another £600 from? 'God has not failed to provide for us, all through,' they said. 'The money will come.' Insurance paid up, and local women ran a jumble sale to cover the difference.

The two stories are repeated in different forms all around the Mission. It makes you think! What are we supposed to say about inner city ministry? That we are knights in shining armour, riding out against the enemy? That we are deeply sensitive human beings, open to everyone? That we are forever 'outsiders', because we try to make a difference? That we are just there as fools, being used?

Or that we are only half-believers, held by a kind of self-deception to a vocation only really half in our guts? That we are diminished by the smallness of our calling? That we sometimes dread the thought of coming back? That when we are away, there is a kind of inner groaning within us, till we get back to the smell of curry, the unkempt gardens, the tin cans in the street, the shifty, covered figures of fearful people silently going about their business of survival and the search for some spark of significance?

Or that we sometimes feel gutted, too vulnerable, too besieged, too used, too much open to whatever and whoever comes, too uncritical, too undemanding, too naive, laughed at, mocked, crucified? In the midst of a period when local youngsters were vandalizing the building and physically attacking the flat residents, the minutes of the Grimesthorpe Church Meeting for 25 July 1993 refer to Louise Gough's not wholly tongue-in-cheek 'devotional verse for meditation', which was I Kings 19.10: 'I am left all alone, and they are trying to kill me.' I sometimes wonder whether it was any different for Jesus. He certainly was vulnerable, besieged, used. And he certainly needed just to get away from it all. Right at the beginning of his ministry, in Mark 1. 35–38, we read:

> In the morning, while it was still pitch black, Jesus got up and went to find a deserted place. And he was there, praying. But Simon and his companions hunted him out. When they found him, they said to him, 'Everyone is searching for you.' He replied, 'Let's go to some other towns. I need to proclaim the message there. That is what I came to do.'

Soon after, when Jesus got back to Capernaum, and got into his own house (Mark 2.1), people besieged him there, inside and outside his house. Finally, frustrated people even took the roof off the house to get at him (Mark 2. 3–4).

Jane describes her 'incarnational' ministry thus: 'We are

learning everything from the local people. We come in as a child. We thought we could come and do something. But we can only be ourselves. Transformation is about becoming relational – and I have to do that first myself.'

'What makes my presence here acceptable,' says Jane, 'is just my being here. My stuff gets stolen. My plants get nicked. My door has eggs thrown at it. My sleep is broken by rows outside, or noisy radios, or cars racing by. Whatever happens to them, happens to me. And whatever they do, I'll still be here.'

If you are really incarnational, it means enfleshment. You are putting flesh around a presence which is more than your own. Immediately you come in, compelled by God-presence within, being filled with the fullness of God (Eph. 3. 18), then that position determines your way. That means 'day by day picking up the cross' (Luke 15. 4). The reality of Jesus' cross is that he not only carried it, but fell under it. He could not carry the cross. Someone else had to do it, Simon of Cyrene (Luke 20. 1–5). Jane comments:

> Enfleshment does not automatically make you acceptable to the people where you are enfleshed. You are not incarnating yourself into their flesh. You are enfleshing God's presence in yourself and the world, in their place. Being incarnate does not necessarily give you a place within the locals' understanding. Jesus was not understood or accepted in the places he was incarnate. He was used there. We must not confuse seeking to identify with the Way of Christ in an area with being accepted by the people.

Jesus says the Kingdom is like a woman who takes a tiny bit of yeast, and puts it into the dough, until the whole mix is leavened (Luke 13.21). We are meant to be like the yeast. But, says Jane, 'If we are, then we are in the dough – to be kneaded, pummelled, stretched out, turned over, rolled over, then cut up, put into an oven and baked. And at the end, all that happens to us is that we are devoured by others. Other people come and eat us! Only when there is death to the yeast as yeast is there life for the dough as dough. And only when the dough as loaf dies, and is consumed, is there the purpose of the whole operation, life for other people.'

The model of the incarnation is, of course, for disciples. Everyone does not need to be yeast, or salt, or the light, or the grain of mustard seed. But those who are called to be disciples must be prepared to be used, pummelled, distorted, hurt and abused. For they are being used as the Son of Humanity, the 'Suffering Servant' who brings life to others (Mark 10. 45) and whose life and blood and energy are for the shalom of the city and the peace of the nations.

The incarnate community makes its own converts. Into community houses, lonely bedsits, tower block maisonettes, they come in their ones and twos. Ruth Ward was training for the Methodist ministry at UTU, and had a placement at The Furnival. In the summer 1998 edition of *Magnet*, the Methodist women's Network magazine, she writes:

> The most important thing Jane has done, by living with the people of the estate, is to show them that they are valuable people, whom she loves and believes in, and whom God loves and believes in too.
>
> As I watched Jane at work, and became involved myself, my vision of ministry was turned on its head. I thought of Jesus, who spent his ministry eating with people, listening to them, and telling stories – Immanuel, God with us, living, breathing, laughing, weeping with us; connecting people to each other, to themselves and so to the ever-powerful love of God.

Ruth decided to change her ministerial calling so that she could become a Minister in Local Appointment on the Fairfield estate in Buxton, where her home is. Here, from an Ashram Community-related shop/flat/base, she now also exercises an incarnational ministry.

What authenticity can there be for incoming vocational, professional people, like myself and Grace? When you have been in a place for thirty years, it is hard to think of yourself as an 'incomer'. The events of every day become the background to one's life. One day, a police car arrived outside the house opposite where I live. Two policemen went into the men's lodging-house opposite. Immediately, six Pakistani youths, five Afro-Caribbean youths and a couple of white kids were around the police car, running up and down, questioning two more police-men who also arrived.

We're a cosmopolitan street, Edwardian terraced houses one side, 1930s semis on our side. Opposite, house by house, there's a retired white lecturer, an Afro-Caribbean hospital sister, an Afro-Caribbean Seventh Day Adventist pastor, a Pakistani taxi driver, each with their families. And then beyond it, a hostel, and more Pakistani families. The houses on our side are set back, above the road. Grace and I bought our house in 1991, when it was clear that we preferred to settle where we had been for twenty years – and after we had tried for a disastrous short year to live out in the country! Our eldest son, Chris, also lives with his family on Abbeyfield Road. It is a tolerant neighbour-hood. People get on with their own lives, but they know their neighbours, and act together occasionally.

For Grace and myself, it is clear that a vocation to the city is a matter of long-term commitment. For sure, the city is not the place for the short-term incomer. We need people who will come and stay. In a document on ministry in SICEM, pro-duced in December 1994, the then Team Ministry meeting (Duncan, Inderjit, Peter Habeshaw and myself) said:

> The minister is the only full time employee, free to pick up and service special needs or campaigns or schemes as they arise. The minister must organize and see through whatever is entrepreneured! Ministry is the out-runner, the MC, the Chancellor of the Exchequer, and the backstop, not for all SICEM work (there is an excellent Finance Group), but for projects as they arise. And projects are an essential part of SICEM, or we cease to be a 'mission'. And projects help to keep the SICEM branches going.

Whether ministers or anyone else, what we need in the city is more 'social entrepreneurs'. Some social entrepreneurs are there already within local neighbourhoods. Occasionally, they can be those who are initially 'incomers'. Best of all, the two groups learn, sometimes quickly, sometimes slowly, to be entrepreneurs together.

# 18

# Counting the Cost

## – and Jesus' Advice to Would-be Missioners

'Domestic housekeeping' is often not the most exciting part of a community's life. But equally, you can gauge the ethos and philosophy of an institution or group by the way they conduct their internal business, finance their affairs, and contribute together to the common cause. So, this chapter is about the internal economics and policy-making of SICEM – in the belief that some important principles are embedded here.

The treasurers and administrators and planners of Christian mission have a striking saying of Jesus in Luke 14. 31–33 to start them off:

> Consider a king going to war against another king.
> Will he not first of all sit down and consider whether he is able with his ten thousand men to overcome his opponent who comes with twenty thousand?
> If he cannot do so, then, while the other is still far away, will he not send a delegation and try to negotiate terms of peace?

The dramatic little story of the king who has to face facts is used by Luke as an illustration of the way that would-be disciples must 'count the cost' before they go for discipleship, and consider all its implications – for father and mother, wife and children, brothers and sisters, and above all, their own life (v. 26). Says Jesus, there is a cross to be carried (v. 27). Only when you consider all this can you build the house of discipleship (vv. 28–30) or join the army of Jesus!

There is a real paradox here. Perhaps 'faith' means going out and meeting armies, not knowing what will happen, 'being a fool for Christ's sake'. But 'working for the Kingdom' means counting the costs, and not letting people down. 'Faith' is acting in the absence of proof and security. 'Working for the Kingdom' is making sure you have adequate provisions when you see a particular task looming up.

You need both in the mission of Christ. But you might not have both at the same time. We see the value of both in our experience in SICEM. 'Faith' is the necessary start-up willingness to go out into the unknown, to back the wrong horse, to stand by unlikely prospects, to dream dreams on the basis of imagination and daring. That's been a part of our life, and is a necessary part of any inner city mission, I fancy. But then 'counting the cost' is the necessary nitty-gritty of practicalities, people and money that have to be considered before you go into a particular project. Are we the right people? Is this the right place? Can we persuade any backers? Are there others who would do it better? Is it our distinctive charism? Is it someone else's? What partners can we find?

All of this has meant endless agony and concern about two things – money and ministry. It's essential to see some of this nitty-gritty. Probably, it accounts for the fact that SICEM has many admirers, but so far, no imitators! Maybe the cost – the stress, the uncertainty, the 'flexibility', is too great for some – what an American ministerial colleague described as 'long-term commitment with short-term financing'.

Early on, it emerged that the small churches could not survive alone or in SICEM simply by the giving of their members. This meant, first, that we had to seek outside financial help, which since 1971 has come through Methodist Home Mission Grants, supplemented more recently by URC grants and, with reference to The Furnival ministry, Baptist grants. But it meant, second, that we needed to produce much more money ourselves. So we tried to move towards the principle first stated in 1974; that all church buildings should as far as possible not only not be a drain on giving, but should become the sources of finance.

This proved more easy to achieve in the newer buildings. The new Pitsmoor building in 1975 was built to make letting out offices possible to create income, and a local doctor's surgery operated there for many years. But elsewhere, renting out premises proved difficult. So another line emerged. The existence of the Ashram Community House from 1971 to 1981 led us into thinking, why could we not have residence as part of our church premises? This would provide three things: first, a place for volunteer workers to live, and use their gifts in the local community and church; second, rents as an income to keep the church going: third, security for the building and a real human presence in it.

So, in 1979 Grimesthorpe sold Wesley Hall and bought a Corner Shop with a flat above, with room for three residents. In 1982, part of the solution to the grave buildings problem at Wincobank was to get money together (including a generous grant of £10,000 from the Anglican Church Burgesses) to alter radically the old Schoolmaster's House, and to make it into a community house for five members. In 1987, Ashram Centre and New Roots shop was opened with room for three residents. From 1973 to 1991, UTU bought five houses, partly so as to have security of income from rents even if there were not enough students coming. In 1996 and 1997, Ashram Community bought two houses in Rock Street.

The only other notable income into SICEM church buildings was earned between 1981 and 1988, when our Manpower Services Scheme Community Programme brought in rents and made possible considerable alterations and improvements. The largest result of this was at Wincobank, where a whole new storey was added in the Sunday School.

Ministers, similarly, earn money for SICEM so that SICEM can pay them! Whatever I spent my time doing had to provide part of my finance. Partly, this was because the only way to be fair to small struggling churches paying their assessments of money was to ensure that whatever else I used my time for would also pay for that time. Thus, from 1972 to 1997, Ashram Community nationally contributed to SICEM because of my work as its leader, as did the Eucharist Congregation from 1974 till 1997, and the New Roots shop and Ashram Centre from 1991 to 1997, not least as our SICEM-financed car mileage included the thrice weekly trips to the wholesale market by Grace. For six years, 1977 to 1983, I lectured in vacations at Drew University in USA, partly as a way of getting basic finance into UTU, which had to get finance into SICEM to pay my Methodist minister's stipend.

The largest local amounts towards salary support have come from Urban Theology Unit. In 1987, when SICEM was not able to get enough money together to pay for the new minister whom four of the churches needed, it was UTU that offered to put in an extra £1,000. UTU has in fact made possible part-time ministries in very small churches which would not have been available on any other basis.

And we cobble together jobs on the basis of bits and pieces from every possible source, to keep the work going, or to develop it. One result was that the newly-opened Foundry Court Housing Association complex from 1974 to 1979 had Ian Lucraft as one-third time chaplain resident in its midst, with support from the Methodist Connexional Advance Fund. After that, the newly-opened Lopham Street Community Workshop had a one-third post as co-ordinator, again with Ian. All our ministerial appointments are put together by a mix of income from particular SICEM branches or pieces of work. Thus, ordained ministry is seen not as a gift or imposition by denominations from the outside, but as grass-roots churches and projects collaborating to provide paid ministerial posts. Outside denominational financial help has been crucial, but always in support of local initiatives and local strategizing.

I have thus used my own personal bits of money-making capability to keep the whole thing going. There are no 'perks', very few, and tiny, wedding fees or funeral fees; no hospital chaplaincies. The royalties from my books are given towards the support of the work – in fact to Urban Theology Unit. On reflection this seems an obvious and not special thing. But it illustrates the same point. Ministers in SICEM, like everyone else, contribute as much as they can to the common pool, whereby salaries are also paid. Sometimes, our commitment has to precede finance. Jane Grinonneau offered to come in September 1996 when there was no money at all to pay her. We cobbled together a three-way salary in the end, from UTU for lecturing, from the Barnabas Trust, and finally from the Baptist Union Home Mission Fund, whom Jane persuaded to follow her call with their finance.

In January 1997, we had an open SICEM meeting which we called 'Stargazing'. We reviewed and updated a document of 1987 called 'SICEM in the Nineties', and affirmed again the kind of policies on SICEM itself, the Mission Units, the People and the Work which will be clear from chapters 4 and 15. Both documents also had a section on finance, which in 1997 goes:

SICEM will continue to rely upon the generous giving of all its members, and at least maintain the present levels of local financial support;
* The mission and ministry of SICEM will continue to require the support of denominational funding
* Other sources of funding, especially for particular capital projects, will be vigorously researched
* Where possible, buildings will earn income to support mission projects.

Two unseens need to be added. First, there is complete trust in a small finance group – basically Iain Cloke, Peter Smithies and Barry Swift. Second, the fundamental SICEM 'will to share' means we help each other out. An 'Affirmed Statement' says:

Each unit will make every effort to meet its contribution to the total work of SICEM, but understanding that should this prove to be impossible for any particular unit, it will contribute as much as it is able, and other units acknowledge their commitment to give over and above their 'assessment' in order to show love and concern for colleagues who face special difficulties.

It's all enormously worth doing, but there is a cost to be

counted, a price to be paid. Part of that is in personal commitment, and an effective sign and symbol of that is money.

The last four chapters have been about four elements of our
spirituality and our strategy. But, the reader may say, there is no
spirituality! And very little strategy!

Spirituality is the way you keep yourself together as a disciple
of Christ in the mysteries of being and being there, breathing in
and breathing out, reacting and reflecting, being exposed and
being comforted. Spirituality is not a separate part of discipleship to Jesus. It is not primarily prayers, quiet times, meditation, retreats or worship occasions. Spirituality will probably
take you into all these things, but they will only be the sustaining support systems, which will vary according to your
temperament. They will be different, we have discovered,
depending on your primary Jesus commitment, which is in
terms of your discipleship. Your discipleship is about where
you are, who you are, what you do, with whom you live, why
you do what you do. So you dig deep into what already
convicts, converts, establishes you, into what informs your
discernment and elaborates your commitment, out of the
stories and traditions and communities of Christ. That is your
spirituality – the wells from which you drink, to keep your life
in Christ alive.[1]

And strategy? The Gospel actions on the streets are your
mission, the Gospel twos and threes are your model of the
church, the Gospel calls are your start-ups and your agenda, the
Gospel demands are your insurance and your policy for
personnel. Mission strategy needs doing all over again, starting
here with just these four![2]

# 19

# Seminary of the Streets

## – and the Twelve Appointed to be With Him

One of the classic elements in the cycle of deprivation which characterizes life in deprived city areas is the absence of educational facilities. Local schools are typically underachieving schools. Earl Marshall School, our local secondary school, where my wife Grace taught for ten years, went through a series of tragedies and failures, was one of David Blunkett's eighteen 'named and shamed' schools in 1997, and has now reopened under a new name – Firvale. Meantime, the secondary school where our three, now grown-up, children just about survived – Firth Park – slowly begins to raise its standards.

What is lacking in our areas is not simply adequate schools, but also all the other ancillary educational provisions which exist in more affluent areas. The churches also do not place their educational provisions in poor areas. Our local RC secondary school, De La Salle, was closed in 1976. And the multitude of other facilities linked with churches and church schools and colleges were never here.

One thing the Methodist Church did right when it suddenly had to find a place for me in 1970 was to find an inner city location. For that was obviously where the Urban Theology Unit had to be. In an early article (1977) on 'Alternative Theological Education', I wrote:

Traditional theological education has taken it for granted that it must be 'academically respectable'. It has assumed that the presuppositions, methodologies, personalia, style, career expectations and professionalisms appropriate to the academic world are appropriate for theology. This implies a notion of theology or of Christian studies which places these alongside other 'areas' of knowledge or investigation which can be dealt with in an academic way. Clearly, if Christian theology is basically 'the Christian story and what Christian communities and disciples have done or thought with it' – a working definition – then there are ways of studying it which are and should be similar to those employed in any other study. But that is different from automatically taking the academic milieu, with all its inevitable characteristics, as the appropriate or only way in which theology is to be studied.

The alternative model to academics is discipleship. The typical image of academics is the Professor with his students. The typical image for discipleship is the leader with followers. Thus, W. E. Visser 't Hooft declared at the end of the 1960s that what we needed was a number of 'theological action stations built around a charismatic Socrates'.[1]

This is still UTU's tradition. When asked, 'Is UTU part of Sheffield University?', the proper answer is 'No. The university accredits degrees we teach. But UTU is part of SICEM.' Our first base is in discipleship in the city, and academics are useful to us to deepen and discipline our discipleship, as I hope to show in *Theology from the City*.

So, each Study Year brings a new group of amazingly varied people who have picked up their lives and moved into the inner city to be part of our 'community of study and action', our 'seminary of the streets', our 'people's university'. And often, as I look at them, I reflect on the formation of that archetypal 'community of study and action' – the group of Jesus and his disciples. Often, I have read to the new group the stages of the call of the first disciples in Mark 1. 16–20. Then, a bit later, I have shared the story of Jesus' outline syllabus of the discipleship disciplines of being a group, being with him and being sent out, in Mark 3. 13–14:

> Jesus went up on to a high place,
> and called to him

those whom he had use for,
and they came to him.

And he appointed twelve of them,
in order that they might be with him,
and be sent out
to proclaim the message
and to have authority to exorcise demons.

The formation of a group of committed disciples is always the originating force behind any piece of Christian community. If Mark's Gospel is 'the beginning of the Good News' (Mark 1.1), then every start-up of a Gospel community or a Gospel project is like the call of disciples to leave behind where they've been – fishing, boats, business (see Mark 2.14), and then get behind the Master as followers, and finally pick up a new project – fishing for people.[2] This is the pattern in Mark 1.17, 1.20 and 2.14.

It is the pattern still. Somehow, people in the midst of a thousand other things hear a call, get a nudge, see a possibility, to go to a different place and follow a new Master, and get into a new project. So, the call story of Mark 1. 16–20 is alive and well, here and there. Initially the call is followed just by being with the new Master, wandering around, involving oneself in a few precipitate first actions, like sitting down with tax collectors and sinners (Mark 2. 15–18), or refusing to fast because other people are fasting (vv. 18–20), or being 'acted parables' of pieces of unshrunk cloth (v. 21), or new wine needing new wineskins (v. 22), or people helping themselves to holy food (vv. 23–27).

But then it has to get more serious, for some at least. Putting on the occasional show is fine, going along with the action is fine. But some time there is decision time – or appointment time. The Master has a community to form. He needs committed people – people who will not only follow him, but learn from him, be his companions, sufficiently so that he can in turn send them out to carry to a wider area the message and the action he has himself inaugurated. So Jesus chooses specific people, gives them specific rules to keep, teaches them specific words and actions, so that eventually they can themselves be sent out – as happens a few chapters later in Mark 6. 7–23.

So, UTU today has a double intention – to seek for relevant urban discipleship, and to train people in relevant vocation. As our Mission Statement of 1995 begins:

> UTU seeks to be an Association of Christians from all denominations committed to the search for relevant Christian discipleship in the city, working through its members in many places, sharing their gifts, insights and experiments.
>
> UTU also seeks to be a Community of Study and Commitment based in the inner city, where people can come from many backgrounds, nationalities and traditions, for vocational discovery and theological and ministerial education.

Within these two intentions, the Mission Statement makes heady commitments to 'the radical Gospel', to 'the search for Christian discipleship and vocation in the city', to 'the empowerment of the poor and powerless', to 'the theological and ministerial potential of each Christian', to 'the specific context in which theology, ministry and action take place' and to 'the participation of people in their own education and liberation'.

This is the situation into which people come. They are a mix of people from very diverse backgrounds, with varying educational qualifications, of all ages, races, colours, jobs, denominations, theologies and temperaments. The courses they come on will often give them diplomas or degrees as well as the basic urban vocational and theological orientation. At present, we have a Diploma or Bachelor Degree in Ministry and Theology for basic training for lay or ordained ministry; a Masters or Doctors Degree in Ministry for those already in ministry who wish to deepen their practice and reflection; and a Masters or Doctors Degree in Philosophy for those who want to research and write in urban, contextual or liberation theologies. All our degrees are awarded by Sheffield University.

Since 1991, a small group of students have done their basic
initial training for Methodist ministry with us. One of the
modules they study is called 'Being a Minister'. Christine Jones
co-ordinates the course. I asked her for some reflections on this
task, and on her first year at UTU, 1997–98. What follows is
Christine's response.

One thing which has struck me during the course of this year is
the number of times someone has said to me, 'Will it be safe to
come?' That sentiment has been echoed by other people –
'What on earth is it that makes you come and live and work in
such a place?' One of the answers is almost a trite one, in that I
enjoyed the thought of working here, but there are also other
deeper reasons too.

One of my favourite Bible stories is the woman who anointed
Jesus in Mark 14. 3–9. Jesus goes to share a meal at a Pharisee's
house. He does not receive from his host the common cour-
tesies, but as he is at table, a woman comes and anoints him.
This woman, in the Synoptic Gospels, remains anonymous. In
Luke 7.37, she is described as a sinner. I remember in one Local
Preachers' tutorial group having heated discussions on this
topic. They assumed she was a prostitute. Where in the text
does it say that? But, they came back, surely the words, 'she's a
sinner' are saying she's a prostitute. As if that is the only sin
there is! Those trainee Local Preachers were guilty of *eisegesis*
(reading into the text), no doubt based on things they had read
or heard in the past.

But let's assume for a moment they are right. A woman in
those times was totally dependent upon the men in her family,
first her father and then her husband. If she was orphaned, or
widowed, and no other male in the family was prepared to take
responsibility for her, what was she to do? She could not work,
that was a male prerogative. So if she wasn't allowed to earn
her living honourably, how could she provide for herself? To
me, that says it wasn't necessarily the woman's fault she was a
prostitute, if she was one. It could well have been her society,
her culture which had forced her into that situation.

Her story begins to resonate with *The Full Monty* – filmed around this area. This time it is men who wanted to work, but who were not able to do so, and who in desperation turned to stripping to increase their income. Just as for the woman who anointed Jesus, some of the problems to be found in this community are not necessarily the fault of the people who live here.

*The Cities* Report speaks of some families in areas like this who have not worked for three generations.With the loss of finance and hope and self-esteem that brings, is it any wonder the community is disintegrating? The woman is a paradigm for this area. Here was someone whose life was not easy, but who cared. Yet as she tried to do something, she was condemned and criticized. The Pharisee immediately made assumptions about her. She was not the sort of person he wanted around him – she was corrupt and dangerous and not nice to know.

How often this year I have heard criticisms of this area; assumptions made. Questions like: 'Is it safe to bring the children?' Jesus saw beyond the assumptions, allowed the woman to minister to him, and blessed her for it. Maybe, in part, ministry here is about challenging people's assumptions.

During the year, on the 'Being a minister' course, we have looked at models of ministry. The woman anointing Jesus' feet produces amazing models for ministry.

If the job is being done correctly, there will be times in ministry when there is opposition and criticism; times when mistakes are made; times when something goes wrong, and you feel embarrassed by it. The woman who came to wash Jesus' feet is a model of courage and determination and love. When we invite someone to dinner, we share together behind closed doors. It is very likely as Jesus shared the meal, they ate outside. Most of the houses were small and dark, and if Jesus was accompanied by the twelve disciples, as is suggested in Matt. 26.8, then it would be very difficult to fit that number into a small Palestinian house. So the chances were that they ate in the courtyard, which would be a semi-public place. As this woman approaches, all eyes turn to her. She was blatantly not welcome. Yet, despite the embarrassment, the feeling that all eyes were upon her, she still goes and anoints Jesus' feet. That says something to me about ministry; it is the service of God despite the opposition, despite the consequences, despite what people will say. And that is never easy.

As we read the story, we can read it with the gift of hindsight. We know what happened in the end. The woman could not be in that position. How was she to know that Jesus was not going to shout at her, as most men did? How did she know that Jesus was going to accept her actions with the grace that he did? She could only hope and trust in the knowledge that she already had of him. In a way, the woman's action was not an appropriate one. It was flamboyant and dramatic. It was not without its sexual element, for here she is kissing Jesus' feet and wiping them with her hair. How is Jesus supposed to respond? Ministry is sometimes about trial and error. If mistakes are not made then we are avoiding decisions and action. If everyone assures us we are doing well, then we are not facing conflict or the difficult issues.

This woman may not have acted wisely or appropriately, but the motivation was right, and Jesus blessed that. Somehow that too would seem to be a model for ministry – a model which says that at times we will mess things up, we may react to situations in inappropriate ways. But Jesus remains there for us and still accepts our service. There is, though, a flip side – that there will be times when others behave inappropriately towards us – and how do we then manage that?

A seminary of the streets has to be a seed bed for people's lives and ministries. The word seminary itself comes from the mediaeval Latin word *seminarium*, which means a seedplot, a place to nurture seeds. The plotting and planting and nurturing of seeds, and the care of them as they begin to sprout, is a fascinating and thrilling business to be engaged in, and to do it in and for the world of cities is humbling and demanding and infinitely rewarding.

So, we look for people to come and be part of the seed-bed of radical change, of eye-opening, of conscientization. Every

August for the past twenty years UTU has published this advert in the religious press:

### UNIQUE OPPORTUNITIES

Every year, people young and old, looking
for challenging discipleship,
find their way to the Urban Theology Unit
for its Study Year, and to the
Sheffield Inner City Ecumenical Mission
for its Community Houses, Projects
and Centres.
Write to us with details about yourself!

The invitation is still open![3]

# PART FOUR

# HOPES AND PROSPECTS

*Hearing It Again for the Future of Our Cities*

*We have a dream, we have a dream*
*This nation's folk both black and white,*
*Will sit together at the Feast*
*As sons and daughters in God's sight*
*We have a dream, we have a dream*
*That North and South, both rich and poor,*
*Will hear the message of the Christ*
*That all must share God's harvest store.*
*We have a dream, we have a dream*
*That from the mountain of despair*
*A stone of hope can still be hewn*
*To build a land that's just and fair.*
*We have a dream, we have a dream*
*That love and justice have no bounds*
*Harmonious songs will soon transform*
*This nation's wild, discordant sounds.*
*For Christ has called us to be one*
*Let barriers now be broken down,*
*Let freedom ring from every hill*
*In every village, every town.*

Martin Eggleton

# 20

# People and Problems – Again

In this chapter, I return to issues about the ways we as a nation deal with the cities. What conclusions are to be drawn from our experiences and stories, concerning the deprivations and disadvantages highlighted in chapter 2, and referred to in the chapters of Part Two?

As we have seen, the Good Samaritan approach alone cannot solve the endemic problems of the people and the neighbourhoods in our cities. Every small piece of work must be related to the solution of the larger problems. But we can now say that the larger solutions must be based on the discoveries and the people of the small solutions. Everything hangs together. The cycle of deprivation must be broken wherever it can be, for individuals, small groups and specific communities. Equally, we must demand and work for a vision of a new city which totally replaces that cycle. *The Cities* Report tried to take up the 'cycle of deprivation' problem, and to substitute a 'virtuous circle'[1] in which one positive element tends to reinforce another. The six elements in the 'virtuous circle' are:

A greater sense
of community

Economic prosperity
and vitality

A clean, sustainable
environment

An equal, socially
just society

Churches with an
enhanced role

Personal security
in safer cities

Only when ways have been found to deal with all these elements together can the power systems and controlling policies which determine and secure the continuance of the cycle of deprivation be overcome. The government's Social Exclusion Unit, established in Autumn 1997, concentrated on three projects – school truancy, people sleeping rough, and disadvantaged housing estates. We await the policy changes, and wish them well. But how will each 'solution' relate to the whole? The September 1998 Report, *Bringing Britain Together*[2] is subtitled 'A National Strategy for Neighbourhood Renewal', but it is not yet clear how the nineteen 'pathfinder' authorities will produce the kind of policies which the government will apply in every needy area.[3]

Our *Cities* Report is full of suggestions and examples for public policy. They still await the attention they deserve. The Report precedes its recommendations with this sobering comment:

> We find it impossible to be entirely confident about the future of Britain's cities. The Working Group's reservations derive from two main factors: first, an awareness of the sheer scale of the economic forces now affecting Britain's cities; and second, a doubt, based on past experience, as to whether any Central Government will have the political will to create the necessary framework of policies and resources, to enable our cities to move confidently into the future, as prosperous, socially just, sustainable and safe places within which to live and work.[4]

In the year after *The Cities* Report was published, in 1997–98, four of the Working Group, including myself, had consultations involving church and political leaders, up and down the country. I was responsible for eight in the east and north of England. We held one in Sheffield, which involved the new RC Bishop, John Rawsthorne, the Labour Council leader, Mike Bower, and our own Central Ward MP, Richard Caborn. Richard, who grew up in our area, had joined us for the Palm

Sunday 1996 Walk from Lopham Street Church (he was in their football team as a youth) to The Furnival.

I recalled the many campaigns and meetings when I had joined with Richard, and with David Blunkett, over the years. Richard talked at length of what had been done and what would be done in his work as Minister for the Regions.

'Everything has changed,' he ended.

'Richard,' I said, 'nothing has changed!' I went on, 'Down here at the bottom, everything is exactly the same as it was. We have yet to see any change.'

I reminded the meeting that our Report on *The Cities* called for specific responses by government and local authorities, including:

1. Abandon the 'lottery' of wasteful competitive bidding systems for grants, especially in the Single Regeneration Budget.

2. Build calculations of the social, community and environmental costs of policies into all plans for 'regeneration'.

3. Adjust spending targets to deal with the complex of government departments which secure the continuance of the 'cycle of deprivation' in some urban areas. Health, education, social services, and community services all need to be considered as parts of a single whole.

4. Legislate for equal shares in 'partnership' between government, local authority, business, voluntary sector and local community groups.

Well, the new regulations for the Single Regeneration Budget look a considerable improvement but are still based on a competitive system capable of abuse. The Green Paper on Welfare is good on analysis, but light on solutions. The New Deal has helped some people, but does not tackle the long-term unemployed, and still puts its products at the mercy of the vagaries of the economy.

The government's comprehensive spending review of July 1998 promised for the three year period 1998–2001 the provision of £3.6 billion on renewing housing stock and £800 million on a New Deal for Communities, tackling unemployment, crime, and poor education on selected key poor housing estates. Also, the education budget of £19 billion includes £540 million for the Sure Start programmes for under-threes in 250 deprived areas. There is £188 million more for drug prevention and treatment, and an extra £300 million for policing. David Blunkett wrote to me in February 1999:

> We really are already seeing a difference. Education is improving, the kids are learning to read, we have the Education Action Zone from Burngreave northwards up and running, Fir Vale School has got more than double the number of first preferences for this September than last year and we have got a Health Action Zone for Sheffield. What I am looking for now is to get a real Single Regeneration Budget programme up and running in the north of the city, but I am also looking to ensure that the good start we have made for the New Deal for the young unemployed, is carried forward vigorously.

By December 1999, around 200,000 youngsters nationally have entered the New Deal and 145,000 of them have found work.[5]

All of these are very welcome policies and achievements of government. Yet, as David says in his Foreword, the people in the deprived communities must grow, respond and take control. I believe, fundamentally, that the style and method, the people and the projects, of the grass-roots communities related on these pages, are paradigms of what has to work politically, both in local politics and in national politics. This means that the political institutions and leaders in our nation and in our cities have to learn from the people and the programmes of the deprived neighbourhoods and their communities, not the other way round.

One specific point has become more and more clear to me, in the period after *The Cities* Report. One of our recommendations says:

> It is important to make good the current deficit in local

democracy. This could be achieved by: increasing the proportion of local expenditure which is locally determined;
restoring to local authorities some of the responsibilities
which have been removed from them during recent years;
and considering the benefits of developing more active,
local democratic mechanisms, such as citizens juries, local
referenda and neighbourhood councils.[6]

This needs elaborating. The time has come when those of us
committed in local community initiatives must demand our
proper place in local government. Single Regeneration Budget
bids do now involve local groups, and this is sometimes well
done, as in our local Burngreave Community Action Forum,
which brings together around thirty local groups, and works
hard as our umbrella for local interest groups – or at least does
so for the current bid.

But we have not yet tackled the problem of genuine grass-
roots democracy within the neighbourhoods or areas of our
cities. This emerged as a key issue at the London Consultation
of the British Council and One World Action in April 1998.
The theme was 'Breaking New Ground – Governance and
Civil Society: New Roles, New Relationships'. I proposed
that we work at models for local neighbourhood government.
For a start I suggested a check list for neighbourhood government:

   1. There must be a clear crisis situation which demands
special attention and solutions, deriving from street-level ongoing involvement by people actually participating in the situation.

   2. There must be a clear function and role which grass-roots
government fulfils. There must be responsibilities and powers
which this level has which are different from what local or
national government provide.

   3. There must be a clear model, a structure and constitution,
with lines of answerability to a major outside body independent
of but relating to national and local government.

   4. There must be money available, concerning which the

grass-roots organization has decisive power. Something from outside has to be fed in as a radical new element.

5. There must be 'social capital' which participants in the process achieve. This is often initially by the 'gift' of middle-class people saying that local people will have power, and facilitating this. But it moves over into genuine locally owned power.

Community cannot be achieved simply by government, at whatever level, I said. Some local projects with minimal economic bases are needed.

On 30 July I found my long time campaigning contemporary, Bob Holman from Glasgow, making the point sharply in a *Guardian* response to the Open Letter from 150 welfare academics to Alistair Darling as new Social Services Minister. Bob Holman wrote:

> The letter from 150 welfare academics to Alistair Darling is to be welcomed (Society, July 29). But it, like the government green paper, says not a word about agencies at the hard end. They appear beyond the interest of highly paid ministers and beyond the experience of academics.
>
> Neighbourhood groups and community projects involve over 2 million residents in food co-ops, credit unions, play schemes, day care, community cafes etc. In deprived areas they are a daily support to low income families. The projects have local participation and commitment, but despite a recommendation by the Social Justice Commission, the government refuses to establish a national means of funding them.

What is certain is that there will be no total solutions or political policies which will be able remotely to deal with the endemic deprivations of our cities which does not work with, support and enhance this vast company of committed individuals and groups who work alongside the needy in our time. This book has only told the stories of a few such in Sheffield – there are many other stories, like those of the Sheffield Churches Homelessness Forum, or the Sheffield Vulnerable People's Task Force, or the recently formed Emmaus Sheffield Project, which could be added.

At present, such committed individuals and groups are terribly vulnerable to the ever-changing policies of central and local government. Local authority support for many youth, family and community projects has long since disappeared as the victim of 'cuts', which seem always to be at the expense of the most vulnerable, the volunteer-led or the locally based. In 1989, the Department of Health scheme, Opportunities for Volunteering, helped us establish the co-ordinator's post for the SICEM community work. In 1999, two of our proposed projects have come unstuck, as they were designed with that scheme, suddenly ended, as partner and joint employer. This happens all the time. We spend months on applications, only to find that the goal-posts have been shifted, or the playing field closed down.

It all has to be turned upside down. Hope for our cities comes from heeding signs of hope from the city. As a nation, we need to learn how to extend and magnify the kind of grass-roots processes and programmes which have been described here, not close them down. We need local, self-dependent businesses and community enterprises which keep money circulating within deprived areas – 'third wave regeneration', on the model of our local credit unions.[7] It is not primarily the much vaunted but seldom demonstrated 'good practice', so dear to the hearts of the social scientists, that will save us. Rather, our cities will be saved through the endless, patient, believing sowing of seeds of kindness, consideration, common feeling and imagination, embodied in neighbourhood groups, organizations and businesses, and woven into the support and expectations of long-term leaders and operators whether local or imported in the communities themselves. New economics and politics, bottom-up, is our greatest need. And only when we see it as vitally necessary will we discover how to do it.

In February 2000, Burngreave became a 'New Deal for Communities' area, so it's all up for grabs, now![8]

# 21

# Seekers and Stories – Again

Looking back on our experiences in this book, I now want to invite the reader to reflect on the 'theological practice' I have tried to describe. Picking up the people and issues of chapter 3, what answers have we discovered? What has happened to discipleship? What has happened to theology? What do we have to say to those who might be looking for what to do with their lives? What might we suggest to those trying to get together a view of what Christianity is all about?

With regard to discipleship, we have met groups and individuals who plainly see their being in the city, and their prophetic and servant ministries there, as a necessary and proper way to be Christian disciples. This must pose the question for others seeking appropriate discipleship:

If discipleship means these things,
    to these people, in this place,
Does it mean I can live a similar discipleship
    with my people, in my place,
Or do I have to find new people and places
    to live this kind of discipleship?

Obviously, our experience is that of being a place where people see and hear the call to radical discipleship, which affects lifestyle, residence, career, profession, friends, culture and future. It is, as the stories have told, a joyful discipleship. But it is joy in the midst of shared experiences, shared situations and shared communities. It is not a joy despite the places and the happenings, but a joy that comes – at times! – through them.

This produces its own versions of spirituality, which arise out of and thus support this kind of discipleship. The Gospel stories, then, provoke conscious and intentional discipleship. Jesus, by his singular concentration on certain ways of behaviour, confines the realm of God to quite specific actions – healing, forgiving, demon-exorcism, power-exposure, enemy-confrontation, disciple-calling, community-building. This is his 'project'. And he calls others to join him in these actions. In contemporary theology, it is mainly the theologians of liberation who have continued this practical, down-to-earth committed discipleship in the places of the radically deprived. This is the way of discipleship, the way of intentional and mainly conscious involvement in the divinely-blessed Jesus actions.

However, the Gospel stories and these Jesus/disciple actions also indicate things about the whole of life. I would put it this way. The Gospel stories are dramatic instances of the way that truth or reality or significance are given to human life. Jesus by his activity indicates and achieves a new situation. Human beings can now act before God in simplicity and joy, because their actions already have within them elements of God's blessing. This is the mystery whereby any people at any time may enter into the divine activity of the Son of Man, Jesus. They do this by acting out or participating in the kind of practice that Jesus was occupied with.

Most people do not intentionally involve themselves in anything which could remotely be called conscious Christian discipleship. For them, the entry into significance occurs, I believe, in the way Jesus indicated in his actions and then his parables. The parables have many different layers, but one layer is certainly that ordinary people in everyday life find themselves in the midst of predictable happenings suddenly stumbling into wholly unpredictable outcomes. And Jesus says the Kingdom of God is like this.

What this means, I think, is that the parables show not only that people in otherwise unremarkable lives can suddenly participate in realities which are also Kingdom realities, but also that the nature of those Kingdom realities can be declared.

And this revealed purpose or significance turns out to be remarkably like the activity of Jesus which we have described – healing, standing by the poor, calling people to radical change, raising up the fallen, leading the powerless into power, challenging those in power, opposing the enemies of the people.

What do our stories and experiences mean for Christian theology? Obviously, all the theology we have done here is based on our own situation. We do not presume to do theology for anyone else. But this needs to be developed. I will develop it in three directions, each of which is a call at least to myself to do more work and writing!

First, we want to be really bound by our situation and really press it, to discover what is going on there, and to receive new insights through it. We want to feel its special possibilities. But that is only possible when we have truly become subject to its special restrictions, problems and limitations. UTU's 'Situation Analysis' is a classic and, in my experience, essential tool in the process of discovering one's context. Theologically, every action of God took place in a context, so we study each context very carefully. The same is true today. God acts in our contexts. God's ongoing incarnation in us is within us as we are, where we are. Wherever we are, we need to see how our context influences or determines our discipleship and our theology, and work for more pluralistic but also critical ways of describing discipleship and doing theology. For myself, this means especially writing up my work in relationship to discipleship in the New Testament, especially Mark's Gospel, which I started in *Disciple and Lord* (1976), *Mark at Work* (1986), *Radical Jesus* (1986) and *Discipleship in the 90s* (1991).[1]

The second reason why we want to press the theological significance of our experiences is that we want to speak to our brothers and sisters in similar situations to ours. We want to make sense to those who share our kind of locations and our commitments. We want to say to people elsewhere in the urban wildernesses, 'Is there anything here that is any good to you – that makes sense of where you are, and your mission – and that could enhance your view of God and reality, your theology?'

Here, I see this as part of the colleagueship of urban practitioners, which comes not least through the present UK Urban Congresses (Liverpool 1995, Belfast 1998, Leeds 2001), the International Urban Ministry Network (Nairobi 1996), Urban Theologians International, the newly formed Urban Theology Collective and occasions like the autumn 1999 Urban Programme at St Deiniol's Library, Hawarden.[2] Some of that experience will be in my later publication *Theology from the City*, alongside the 'theological practice' that we have worked at in UTU.[3]

Third, of course, we want to be heard by people in other contexts. For a start, we want to be heard by people in the academic, middle-class, affluent, Western, and Western-style context. We want to be heard there because much theology in Britain is done by people in that context, and it is always assumed that it is the only 'academically respectable' place in which to do theology. The context of the urban is now decisive for more and more people. But so, too, are other contemporary contexts. We need more 'urban theologies'. But we need other theologies from other contexts. The whole area of contextual and liberation theologies needs much more development. As I think it is about rediscovering an essential part of Christianity itself, I shall continue to pursue this area.[4]

So, we want to be heard by people in the rest of Christendom! We do not want to be imitated by them. We do not want them to say, 'Great, we've all now got to be urban theologians.' No, please do not do that. We have been provoked into doing our theology quite considerably by people in radically dissimilar situations. The German university teachers put forward particular world-views which reflected their situation, and this is also the world we share. The South American priests and pastors operated on the basis of their need to see the actions of God on their streets, so their theology is useful to us. The feminist theologians have taught us always to begin within, with human realities. The writers talking about the postmodern situation are our friends, too, as they are trying to make sense of the fragmentedness, pluralism, incoherence and yet vitality of the contemporary world which is our experience. So, too in the end, urban theology has to constitute clear options and clear contributions alongside other theologies, from which it learns, and alongside which it has to make its distinctive contribution.

The best way to affirm situation-influenced theology is not by imitating our version, but by being provoked by it into demanding that every person's own situation shall also have its situation-influenced theology. Just as the best way to affirm our situation-influenced discipleship is not by imitating it, but by following through the logic and challenge of the Gospel's 'outworkings' in every place, for every person. The stories in this book indicate how the 'outworkings' method gives us a new grasp on reality.[5]

I believe that there is new hope for Christianity itself in Britain, through the discoveries and experiences of Christians like those described in this book. Too many people turn away from Christianity, or never think it worth taking seriously, because they have never seen or encountered anything radically alternative enough to be worth calling 'Christian'. There is hope from the city for tired Christians and even theologians! Here are people who take the way of Christian discipleship as a way meant to be lived in every part of their lives – *who* they see themselves as, *where* they become incarnate, *with whom* they place themselves, *for what* they give their lives. There is hope for the future for Christianity if it becomes again a radical alternative of costly and relevant discipleship, lived out in love and faith wherever there is human need. The little communities and people of the inner cities are signs of hope for all.

# 22

# Communities and Churches – Again

What are the implications of our encounters for the life of community groups and churches? Having lived with the situations and people we were introduced to in chapter 4, and seen them at work, what has to be learned for us all? How do the people of hope whom we have seen chart the future hope for the cities at large?

First, there are surely implications about where people with conscience, the Christians and the churches ought to be putting their resources. Something has to be done, immediately, and by whoever is prepared to do it, to help meet some of the pressing and constant threats to humanity and human wholeness that exist today in our cities. The situation of single parents, the lone old people, the deprived kids, the footloose teenagers, the racial ghettos, the racist groups, the unemployed, the exploited, the drug-pushers, the prostitutes, the handicapped, the homeless, the isolated, the discarded, and the stunted at least deserves to be taken seriously by responsible and sensitive people in our society as the massive human problem which it is.

I get angry when armchair critics seek to minimize the commitment of individuals and groups who get on with some practical action alongside one of these disadvantaged groups. 'You're only doing ambulance work,' they say. Nowadays, I reply, 'If you are lying on the side of the road, beaten, robbed, half-dead, the only thing you need is an ambulance. You don't need some clever long-term cure-all reorientation of public services. You just need some individuals who will come down where you are, and help you in your distress.' It's like the Good Samaritan in Luke 10. 29–37. He could easily have said that the

Jewish systems of care needed overhauling. He didn't. He did what was needed for the man fallen among thieves, and thus proved himself a neighbour, no doubt much to the surprise of the victim, whose own fellow clan members had left him where he was, in order to fulfil the larger requirements of society.

Of course, being a Good Samaritan is not the whole of it. As Ann Morisy's book title says, we need to move 'beyond the Good Samaritan'.[1] But the Good Samaritan is still stage one. The people in need cannot wait for total solutions. Neither can the people with a conscience, or, better, a heart. They see the needs and the needy person, judge the person to be a brother or sister in need, and act on their conviction. We need more people who will see, judge and act in this way. Of course, they do not need to be Christians. Many of them are not. They just need to be sensitive, humane, imaginative men and women. Nor yet are their motives of such great concern. When people need help, they need quite specific pieces of ministry, and provided they are delivered in a straightforward way, what is of first importance is the actual help given, not the attitude of the giver – though most 'do-gooders', as their critics call them, are in my experience a generous and realistic, even self-critical, crowd. If they get their kicks out of helping others, and even like to be rewarded occasionally, what is so wrong with that, compared to the vast majority of people who keep themselves to themselves and never lift a finger to help anyone except those who will help them in return?

In an odd way, the enlightened liberal broad-minded humanist approach of the middle classes, which condemns the do-goodism of the slum-workers, has now become a fashionable right-wing sophistication, which shuts up the doors of mercy, and justifies its self-exclusion and self-centredness by a false modesty, which is really escapism. For Christians, it is also an unwillingness to ask who are the hungry, thirsty, strangers, unclothed, sick or prisoners who are really the hidden Christ (Matt. 25. 31–46). Our stories celebrate a return – or advance – to a more basic, gut-level, hands-on spirituality, which makes sense to people in the cities, and is meant as an invitation to people and politicians more widely.

A second implication of our stories concerns the character of the community's life in these areas. Learn to speak, says Jane Grinonneau, not of the Kingdom of God, but of 'the kin-dom of God'. The Good Samaritan creates a human community of support around the wounded man, in which food, shelter and practical caring go hand in hand. What we need is a multiplying number of sustaining and enriching communities of human companionship. The centrality of eating as the core of being together is a vital aspect of this. 'The messianic banquet' is, as we have seen, a key concept for us. But it has to be a banquet available to everyone. In the July 1998 issue of the SICEM Quarterly magazine, *Here and Now*, Iain Cloke remarks that at Pitsmoor 'It sometimes seems extraordinary just how much of our life and service together is shared around a table, breaking bread together.' He lists: bring and share lunches/teas at meetings, fundraising barbecues, old people's lunches four times weekly, a coffee morning (strawberries and scones), a retreat with friends from St Catherine's, Christ Church and The Furnival, Monday Club's weekend in Hornsea and trip to Cannon Hall Park. Iain concludes:

Of course, a 'food sharing theology' is hardly all that surprising for disciples of our Lord, who himself broke bread and said 'Take and eat; this is my body, broken for you.' We give thanks that at the heart of our fellowship is this sharing in the vulnerability of Christ. So it is that we continue to manifest our commitment to each other and to the community in a sharing of food and friendship, in making ourselves vulnerable to the opportunities and threats of new and deepening relationships.

It is vitally important that this distinctive, human-shaped, communal element be built upon more widely. Inner cities and deprived areas have had millions of pounds thrown at them, and will doubtless get more. But what is really needed is people and communities and money that make the lives of people and communities capable of richness, mutuality, and generosity. Out of these will come enterprise, and self-regard, and contributions to the life of the whole nation. But it is the return of commonness, relatedness, and community which we now know is a basic essential. Churches, voluntary sector, government and local authorities need to start building from this base.

A third lesson to be learned is that we need the distinctive philosophy of constant entrepreneurship, based on the faith, be it secular or Christian, that reform and improvement are constant processes. There are no quick fixes. And there are no permanent solutions. The Christian philosophy is basically that everything has to be changed from the bottom, working upwards. This is totally perverted in the evangelical notion that you must convert people before you can convert systems. The Jesus method is to convert whatever and whoever you can, wherever you can, but realize first that very few people or things will get totally changed, and secondly, that tomorrow it will have to be done all over again, unless the conversion has been to a radically new location and a radically new practice.

So, it's always going back down to the bottom, and starting again. It's always 'keep on rising from the dead'. It's always a new seed being thrust into some new ground. It's always hope being reborn through some new prophetic act. It's always some new 'social entrepreneur' as person, group or scheme. A member of Citizens, a Black Country community organization, put it well at a William Beveridge Convention (*The Guardian*, 11 November 1998):

> We believe that it is never too late. Indeed, all the best things need to have to be re-invented for each new generation. We follow in the footsteps of the Chartists, the dissenters, the trade unionists, and Beveridge.

The hope from the city is that it does all keep happening! There is hope, because it does!

Yes, it is all very small. But it is the smallness of seeds, some-

times being planted against the environment all round, sometimes waiting to be planted when the earth is right – when
money or planners or social and community workers or City
Challenge or Single Regeneration Budget choose to arrive. One
thing is for sure. Money, planners, social and community
workers, City Challenge and Single Regeneration Budget are
totally powerless to turn round the places of disaster and
depression in our cities without the partnership of people and
places already on the ground, which already have local 'street
cred', and already have some commitment and the experience
of trying to do some things. Our Methodist Report on *The
Cities* says that 'Local authorities should identify and support
the network of groups and individuals operating at grass-roots
level,' and that 'The ability to foster and promote this activity is
likely to be crucial for cities' long term economic and social
success.'[2] The 'groups and individuals operating at grass-roots
level' are often Christian ones, and they have the seeds already
for the growth of survival and flourishing in the cities.

The good news for the cities of the present and the future
is that of the new commonwealth of all creation, the sister/
brotherhood of all people. The first seeds of this were in the
practice of Jesus who embodied the new realm – he was 'the
Kingdom in himself', said Origen. Then the seed was carried
round by disciples, and the good news got busy 'bearing fruit
and growing in the whole world, just as in yourselves' (Col. 1.
6). Then the seed got picked up by Christians through the ages.
Now, it is sown by surviving urban people and churches in our
time, and brings forth harvests of hope in the places of despair.

Hardly, I fear, do the churches and most Christians have any
conception of the power of the Gospel seed in their hands. They
have never seen it grow as a whole new way of doing and being
and creating, as it was in the New Testament, and as we have
seen it in the little communities of the city. They have only seen
it, perhaps, as a way to get converts to a basically notional or
convictional Christianity, rather than as a way to secure real
conversions to a total re-orientation of life, place, work and
future.

But the seed is still there, waiting to be used – waiting to be taken again with human hands, heart and head and with the whole body, back down into the ground, back down into the ground especially of the cities of our time, back down into the pains and tragedies and breathless possibilities of the people and places of our contemporary cities.

Take it!

# Notes

*Bible translations and paraphrases are the author's own. The hymns at the head of the four parts of the book are from* Hymns of the City *ed John Vincent, Urban Theology Unit 1989, 1998*

## 1  Seeds in the City

1. *The Cities: A Methodist Report*, Joint Chairs Helen Dent and John Vincent, NCH Action for Children 1997. The booklet *A Cities Workbook*, edited by myself, is a practical guide to local action based on the Report and is available from NCH Action for Children, 85 Highbury Park, London N5 4QQ.
2. John J. Vincent, *Radical Jesus: The Way of Jesus – Then and Now*, Marshall Pickering 1986.
3. John J. Vincent, *Into the City*, Epworth Press 1982.

## 2  People and Problems

1. *Into the City*, pp. 1–32.
2. *Poverty and the Poor in Sheffield*, Sheffield City Council 1993.
3. *Benefits and Poverty in Sheffield*, Sheffield City Council, Corporate Policy Unit 1999; *Area Profiles, 1st Draft*, (1) Brightside, Shiregreen/ Firth Park, (2) Burngreave, Sheffield City Council, Area Action 1999.
4. *Bringing Britain Together: A National Strategy for Neighbourhood Renewal*, Cabinet Office/Social Exclusion Unit 1998, pp. 20, 21.
5. *Poverty and the Poor in Sheffield*, p. 37.
6. Ibid., p. 35.
7. *The Cities: A Methodist Report*, p. 226.
8. Ibid., p. 228.
9. *Eurostat*, European Community, April 1997.

## 3  Seekers and Stories

1. John D. Davies, 'Faith as Story' in *Stirrings: Essays Christian and Radical* ed John J. Vincent, Epworth Press 1976, p. 46.
2. On Gospel Pattern Dynamics, see *Into the City*, *passim*, summary on pp. 106–107. Also Robin Pagan, 'Gospel Patterns' in *Urban Christ:*

*Responses to John Vincent* ed Ian K. Duffield, Urban Theology Unit
1997, pp. 53–65.

3. See my *Radical Jesus* (ch.1, n. 2) pp. 11–86. On this model of Jesus, see
   Laurie Green, 'The Jesus of the Inner City' in *Urban Christ*, pp. 25–33,
   and Chris Rowland, 'Journey Downwards', ibid., pp. 35–46.
4. See my article, 'Imaginative Identification', *Epworth Review*, Vol. 23,
   No. 3, September 1996, pp. 14–20.
5. See my 'An Urban Hearing for the Gospel' in *Gospel from the City* ed
   Chris Rowland and John Vincent, Urban Theology Unit 1997, pp.
   105–116.
6. John J. Vincent, Christine Dodd and Ian Duffield, *Situation Analysis*,
   Urban Theology Unit, revd edn 1998.
7. Cf. my Pastoral Address to the 1990 Methodist Conference, 'The New
   World and the New Christian' in *Discipleship in the 90s*, Methodist
   Publishing House 1991, pp. 3–10.

## 4 Communities and Churches

1. A convenient booklet guide to SICEM is Marian Lowndes, *A Mission
   in the City*, Urban Theology Unit 1988.
2. For further material on the origins and constitution of SICEM see my
   *Into the City*, pp. 25–33.
3. I contrast inner city mission with the central missions in which I
   had previously worked in Manchester and Rochdale in two articles,
   'Strategies for Mission', *Epworth Review*, Vol. 4, No. 2, May 1977,
   pp. 41–50 and 'New Strategies for Mission', *Epworth Review*, Vol. 26,
   No. 2, April 1999, pp. 26–32. On the recent history of urban mission,
   see *The Cities*, pp. 33–44.
4. Duncan Wilson's article, 'Gospel Values in Inner City Churches' in
   *Gospel from the City*, pp. 86–104, is a vivid account of ministry and
   mission in SICEM.

## 5 Palestine and Pitsmoor

1. John D. Davies and John J. Vincent, *Mark at Work*, Bible Reading
   Fellowhip 1986. Cf. esp. pp. 14–18.
2. Ulrich Luz, *Matthew in History: Interpretation, Influence, Effects*,
   Fortress Press 1994. See also his article, 'Kann die Bibel heute noch
   Grundlage für die Kirche sein?', *New Testament Studies*, July 1998,
   pp. 317–39. See also below, ch. 21, n. 5.
3. Cf. Susan Gillingham, *One Bible, Many Voices*, SPCK 1998 or Steven
   Moyise, *Introduction to Biblical Studies*, Cassell 1998.
4. Chris Rowland and John Vincent, *British Liberation Theology* series,

Urban Theology Unit. Titles so far are *Liberation Theology UK* (1995), *Gospel from the City* (1997), and *Liberation Spirituality* (1999). The next volumes are *Black and Asian Theology* edited by Inderjit Bhogal and Lerleen Willis (2000); and *Bible and Practice* ed Chris Rowland and John Vincent (2001).

5. Inderjit Bhogal, 'Grieving in a Multi-Faith Society', pp. 76–85; Jane Grinonneau, 'City Kids as Signs of the Kingdom', pp. 12–29; Jan Royan, 'Nicaragua to the Inner City', pp. 38–51; Duncan Wilson, 'Gospel Values in Inner City Churches', pp. 86–104; John Vincent, 'An Urban Hearing for the Gospel', pp. 105–116. All in *Gospel from the City*.

6. Inderjit Bhogal, 'Prayer, Protest and Politics', pp. 46–60; Jan Royan, 'A Spirituality for Inner City Vocation', pp. 61–67; Grace Vincent, 'Worship at Grimesthorpe', pp. 68–73; John Vincent, 'A New Theology and Spirituality', pp. 95–106. All in *Liberation Spirituality*.

## 6 Poor

1. On Upper Wincobank Chapel, see my article, 'People's Church' in *20/20 Visions* ed Haddon Wilmer, SPCK 1992, pp. 65–81, esp. pp. 73–77.
2. See Bob Holman, *Towards Equality: A Christian Manifesto*, SPCK 1997.
3. Cf. *The Cities*, esp. pp. 55–86.
4. *A Petition of Distress from the Cities* ed John Vincent, Urban Theology Unit 1993. Presented to HM the Queen and Parliament by Kathleen Richardson, Tony Holden and John Vincent, 21 April 1993.

## 7 Excluded

1. There is a Friends of The Furnival organization which sends a Newsletter. Details from The Furnival, 199 Verdon Street, Sheffield S3 9QQ.

## 8 Unemployed

1. Sheffield Employment Bond, Omega Court, 372 Cemetary Road, Sheffield S11 8FT.
2. Sheffield Enterprise Agency, 267 Glossop Road, Sheffield S10 2HB.
3. Sheffield Community Enterprise Development Unit, C28–C33, The Alison Centre, Alison Crescent, Sheffield S2 1AS.
4. Verdon Street Enterprises, 199 Verdon Street, Sheffield S3 9QQ.

## 9 *Immigrants*

1. Inderjit S. Bhogal, 'Grieving in a Multi-Faith Society' in *Gospel from the City*, p. 82.
2. Ibid., p. 80.
3. Ibid., p. 85.
4. Burngreave Community Action Forum and Trust, 12 Burngreave Road, Sheffield S3 9DD.

## 11 *Kids*

1. Current details from Children and Families Project, Shiregreen URC, Valentine Crescent, Sheffield S5 0NX.

## 12 *Handicapped*

1. The 'hermeneutical circle' is used in liberation theology to describe the way that people and projects move from one stage to another. The classic 'hermeneutical circle' is See, Judge, Act, Reflect.

## 13 *Aged*

1. Jenny Hales, *It Were Lovely: Memories of a Super Lady, Florence Harrold*, Grimesthorpe Methodist Church 1992, p. 33.

## 14 *Consumers*

1. Grace Vincent, *New Roots: Shop for Justice*, Ashram Community Trust 1997, from pp. 13–15. From Ashram Community Trust, 178 Abbeyfield Road, Sheffield S4 7AY.
2. See *A Community Called Ashram*, 1995 and *Community Worship 2000*, 1999; both ed John Vincent and published by Ashram Community Trust.
3. For details of Burngreave Ashram and other Ashram Community Projects write to: Community Officer, 178 Abbeyfield Road, Sheffield S4 7AY.
4. See Inderjit Bhogal, 'Participating in Life' in *Wrestling and Resting: Exploring Stories of Spirituality* ed Ruth Harvey, CTBI 1999, pp. 148–53.

## 15 *Telling it the Way it Is*

1. Geoff and Kate King developed this into the 'Dream Scheme' which from 1995 to 1998 operated from Chapel House, Wincobank. The

scheme organizes work projects for young people in environmental, social, creative and personal development, rewarding them with points, to be spent on any leisure, pleasure or sporting activities they choose. Details of twelve current UK schemes from Kate and Geoff King, Dream Scheme Network, 5th Floor, Paragon House, 48 Seymour Road, Manchester M13.

2. The story of the Eucharist Congregation is told in my *Alternative Church*, Christian Journals, Belfast 1976, pp. 60–76 .

3. *Hymns of the City* ed John Vincent, Urban Theology Unit 1989, revd edn 1998.

4. Duncan Wilson, 'Gospel Values in Inner City Churches' in *Gospel from the City*, p. 104.

## 18 *Counting the Cost*

1. On Spirituality, see further my 'Rediscovering Jesus Today' in *Discipleship in the 90s*, Methodist Publishing House 1991, pp. 11–16. Also Jan Royan, above, pp. 91–93; and her article, 'A Spirituality for Inner City Vocation' in *Liberation Spirituality*, pp. 61–67; and my 'A New Theology and Spirituality' in ibid., pp. 95–106. Also Inderjit Bhogal, 'Participating in Life' (see ch. 14, n. 4).

2. In 'New Strategies for Mission' (ch. 4, n. 3), I suggest as strategies for the future: 'Ecclesiolas of Charism', 'A Christianity of Discipleship', and 'Spiritualities of Gospel Coherence'.

## 19 *Seminary of the Streets*

1. John J. Vincent, 'Alternative Theological Education' in *Doing Theology in the City*, *New City* No. 11, November 1977, Urban Theology Unit, pp. 6–8.

2. See 'Getting a Movement Going' in John D. Davies and John J. Vincent, *Mark at Work*, Bible Reading Fellowship 1986, pp. 21–25.

3. The Urban Theology Unit has an open membership, and members receive *UTU News* three times yearly, details of our courses and summer schools, and UTU books and publications as issued. Write to Janet Colby, Urban Theology Unit, 210 Abbeyfield Road, Sheffield S4 7AZ. On UTU's ethos and theology, see further my article, 'An Inner City Learning Community', *The Way*, April 1997, and the forthcoming sequel to the present volume, *Theology from the City*.

## 20 *People and Problems – Again*

1. *The Cities*, p. 88.

2. *Bringing Britain Together: A National Strategy for Neighbourhood Renewal*, Cabinet Office Social Exclusion Unit 1998.

3. See Bob Holman, 'A Voice on the Estate' in *Joined-Up Writing*, Christian Socialist Movement 1999.

4. *The Cities*, p. 215.

5. Statistics from Department of Education and Employment. The National Institute of Economic and Social Research argues that 115,000 would eventually have found jobs, due to the strong economic upswing. 'New Deal Success Inflated', *The Guardian*, 3 December 1999.

6. *The Cities*, Public Policy Recommendations 6.4, p. 231.

7. See further a paper I delivered at the Department of Education and Employment in November 1999, now in 'Regeneration and Community Capacity Building', *Crucible*, July 2000. Also Rob Furbey's paper, 'Urban Regeneration: Reflections on a Metaphor', Centre for Regional Economic and Social Research, Sheffield Hallam University 1999.

8. £20m. is available for Burngreave in the next ten years. 'Burngreave Gets a Lifeline', *Sheffield Telegraph*, 11 February 2000.

## 21 Seekers and Stories – Again

1. John J. Vincent, *Disciple and Lord: The Historical and Theological Significance of Discipleship in the Synoptic Gospels*, Sheffield Academic Press 1976. The other titles are noted in ch. 5, n. 1, ch. 1, n. 2, and ch. 3, n. 7.

2. The Urban Programme, arranged by the Warden, Revd Peter Francis, brought 60 urban ministers and practitioners for short or long periods of study and writing, with myself as part-time consultant. A volume of essays, *Faithless City?*, is to be published.

3. See also Ian K. Duffield, 'Doing Urban Theology' in *Urban Christ* (ch. 3, n. 2), pp. 15–23; Andrew Davey, 'Story-Making: Towards an Urban Hermeneutics', ibid., pp. 47–53.

4. Cf. meantime my article, 'A New Theology and Spirituality' in *Liberation Spirituality* (see ch. 5, n. 4), pp. 95–106; and two pieces in *Reviews in Religion and Theology*: ' "An Interview" with Gareth Jones', August 1996, pp. 82–88; and 'The Challenges and Responsibilities of Contextual Theology', February 1997, pp. 7–13. Also, my article 'Contextual Developing Theologies', *Epworth Review*, Vol. 27, No. 2, April 2000. And a forthcoming volume, *Liberating Christ*, now in progress.

5. The concept of 'outworkings' (cf. ch. 5, p. 40) needs further development, which I plan to attempt in terms of contemporary biblical

studies, as 'Practice Criticism'. See my article 'Outworkings: A Gospel Practice Criticism', forthcoming. Also *Bible and Practice* (see ch. 5, n. 4).

## 22 *Communities and Churches – Again*

1. Ann Morisy, *Beyond the Good Samaritan*, Mowbray 1997.
2. *The Cities*, p. 231.

# Recent Books

This Bibliography mainly covers publications since 1982.
For earlier books under each heading see *Into the City*, pp. 143–46.

## (a) The City

Church, Chris, Cade, Adam and Grant, Adrienne, *Social Exclusion, Poverty and Environmental Action,* Community Development Foundation 1998

Davies, Nick, *Dark Heart: The Shocking Truth about Hidden Britain,* Chatto 1997

Deakin, N. and Edwards, J., *The Enterprise Culture and the Inner City,* Routledge 1993

Girardet, Herbert, *The Gaia Atlas of Cities,* Gaia Books 1992

Hall, Peter and Ward, Colin, *Sociable Cities: The Legacy of Ebenezer Howard,* John Wiley 1998

Hill, Derek, *Citizens and Cities: Urban Policy for the 1990s,* Harvester 1994

Hoggett, Paul, *Contested Communities: Experiences, Struggles, Policies,* Polity Press 1998

Holman, Bob, *Faith in the Poor,* Lion 1998

Jones, Terence, *Britain's Ethnic Minorities,* PSI 1993

Leadbeater, Charles, *The Rise of the Social Entrepreneur,* Demos 1998

Le Gates, Richard and Stout, Frederick (eds), *The City Reader,* Routledge 1996

Pacione, Michael, *Britain's Cities: Geographies of Division in Urban Britain,* Routledge 1997

Rogers, Richard, *Cities for a Small Planet,* Faber 1997

Sandercock, Leonie, *Towards Cosmopolis: Planning for Multi-Cultural Cities,* John Wiley 1999

Sennett, Richard, *Flesh and Stone: the Body and the City in Western Civilisation,* Faber 1997

Sissons, Chris, *Pathways to Local Regeneration,* William Temple Foundation 1998

Vincent, John (ed), *A Petition of Distress from the Cities,* Urban Theology Unit 1993

Walker, Alan and Carol (eds), *Britain Divided: The Growth of Social Exclusion in the 1980s and 1990s*, CPAG 1997

Ward, M., *Rethinking Urban Policy*, Centre for Local Economic Strategies 1994

Warpole, Ken and Greenhalgh, Liz, *The Richness of Cities*, Comedia/ Demos 1999

Willmott, Peter, *Urban Trends*, PSI 1992

Wilkinson, C., *The Drop-Out Society: Young People on the Margins*, Youth Work 1995

*The Cities: A Methodist Report*, Joint Chairs Helen Dent and John Vincent, NCH Action for Children 1997

*The Common Good and the Catholic Church's Social Teaching*, Catholic Bishops' Conference 1996

*Socio-Demographic Change and the Inner City*, Dept of the Environment, HMSO 1995, 1998

*Unemployment and the Future of Work. An Enquiry for the Churches*, CCBI 1997

## (b) Sheffield and Region

Beattie, Geoffrey, *Survivors of Steel City: A Portrait of Sheffield*, Chatto 1986

Green, Alfred, *Growing Up in Attercliffe*, Urban Theology Unit 1981

Hales, Jenny, *It Were Lovely: Memories of a Super Lady, Florence Harrold*, Grimesthorpe Methodist Church 1992

Hey, David, *The Making of South Yorkshire*, Moorland 1979

Hey, David, *A History of Sheffield*, Carnegie Publishing 1998

Jenner, Brian, *The Coal Strike: Christian Reflections on the Miners' Struggle*, Urban Theology Unit 1986

*Benefits and Poverty in Sheffield*, Corporate Policy Unit, Sheffield City Council 1999

*Poverty and the Poor in Sheffield*, Planning Dept, Sheffield City Council 1993

*From Bandstand to Monkey Run: Voices from Firth Park, Shiregreen, Page Hall, Wincobank and Grimesthorpe*, Sheffield City Libraries 1994

## (c) Urban Congregations

Armitage, Michael, *Jesus Loves Brixton, Too*, Marshall Pickering 1986

Blakeborough, Eric (ed), *Church for the City*, Darton, Longman and Todd 1995

Brock, Charles, *Sightings of Hope: Stories of Urban/Rural Mission in the URC*, United Reformed Church 1994

Bunting, Ian, *Claiming the Urban Village*, Grove Books 1988

Calvert, David (ed), *The Outside Church*, Methodist Property Division 1992

Eastman, Michael (ed), *Ten Inner City Churches*, MARC Europe 1988

Halloran, James, *Small Christian Communities: A Pastoral Companion*, Orbis/Columba 1996

Hebblethwaite, Margaret, *Base Communities: An Introduction*, Geoffrey Chapman 1993

Holden, Tony, *Keeping Faith: Ten Years of Inner City Ministry*, Methodist Home Mission 1988

Lockwood, Trevor, *The Church on the Housing Estate*, Methodist Home Mission 1993

Lovell, George, with Garth Rogers and Peter Sharrocks, *The Parchmore Partnership*, Chester House 1995

Lowndes, Marian, *A Mission in the City: The Sheffield Inner City Ecumenical Mission*, Urban Theology Unit 1988

Marchant, Colin, *Signs in the City*, Hodder 1985

Sheppard, David and Warlock, Derek, *Better Together: Christian Partnership in a Hurt City*, Hodder 1988

Vincent, Grace, *New Roots: Shop for Justice*, Ashram Community Trust 1997

Vincent, John (ed), *Community Worship 2000*, Ashram Community Trust 1999

Vincent, John, *Into the City*, Epworth Press 1982

Walsh, Margaret, *Here's Hoping: Heath Town and the Hope Community*, Urban Theology Unit 1991

Wilkinson, John, *The Church in Black and White*, Saint Andrew Press 1994

*God So Loves the City: Seeking a Theology of Urban Mission*, MARC USA 1998

## (d) Urban Mission

Andrews, Dave, *Building a Better World*, Albatross/Lion 1996

Bakke, Raymond, *The Urban Christian*, MARC Europe 1986

Beasley, Mary, *Mission on the Margins*, Lutterworth Press 1996

Bradbury, Nicholas, *City of God?*, SPCK 1990

Green, Laurie, *Power to the Powerless*, Marshall Pickering 1987

Green, Laurie, *The Challenge of the Estates, Strategies and Theology for Housing Estates Ministry*, National Estates Churches Network 1999

Grundy, Malcolm, *Community Work*, Mowbray 1995

Harvey, John, *Bridging the Gap: Has the Church Failed the Poor?*, Saint Andrew Press 1987

Hunter, John, *A Touch of Class: The Story of the Evangelical Urban Training Project*, EUTP 1999

Levin, Hugh (ed), *A Community of Clowns: Testimonies of People in Urban Rural Mission*, WCC 1987

Linthicum, Robert C., *Empowering the Poor: Community Organizing Among the City's 'Rag, Tag and Bobtail'*, MARC USA 1991

Linthicum, Robert C. (ed), *Signs of Hope in the City*, MARC USA 1995

Morisy, Ann, *Beyond the Good Samaritan: Community Ministry and Mission*, Mowbray 1997

Rhodes, David, *Faith in Dark Places*, SPCK 1996

Scott Mayers, E. (ed), *Envisioning the New City: A Reader on Urban Ministry*, Westminster John Knox Press 1992

Villafane, Eldin, *Seek the Peace of the City: Reflections on Urban Ministry*, Eerdmans 1995

Vincent, John, *Starting All Over Again: Hints of Jesus in the City*, WCC 1981

Vincent, John, *Discipleship in the 90s*, Methodist Publishing House 1991

Yamamori, Tetsunao, Myers, B.L. and Luscombe, K.L (eds), *Serving With the Urban Poor*, MARC USA 1999

*Faith in the City: Report of the Archbishop of Canterbury's Commission on Urban Priority Areas*, Church House Publishing 1985

*Living Faith in the City*, General Synod of the Church of England 1990

*Staying in the City: Faith in the City Ten Years On*, Church House Publishing 1995

## (e) Urban Theology

Ahern, Geoffrey and Davie, Grace, *Inner City God: The Nature of Belief in the Inner City*, Hodder 1987

Arbuckle, Gerald, *Earthing the Gospel*, Geoffrey Chapman 1990

Bakke, Ray, *A Theology as Big as the City*, IVP 1998

Beckford, Robert, *Jesus is Dread*, Darton, Longman and Todd 1998

Cohn-Sherbok, D. and McLellan, D. (eds), *Religion in Public Life*, Macmillan 1992

Duffield, Ian K. (ed), *Urban Christ: Responses to John Vincent*, Urban Theology Unit 1997

Green, Laurie, *God in the Inner City*, Urban Theology Unit 1992

Harvey, Anthony (ed), *Theology in the City*, SPCK 1989

Hills, Julian (ed), *Common Life in the Early Church: Essays Honouring Graydon Snyder*, Trinity Press International 1998

Holman, Bob, *Towards Equality*, SPCK 1997

Linthicum, Robert C., *City of God, City of Satan: A Biblical Theology of the Urban Church*, Zondervan 1991

Meeks, Wayne, *The First Urban Christians*, Yale University Press 1983

Murray, Stuart, *City Vision: A Biblical View*, Darton, Longman and Todd 1990

Northcott, Michael, *Urban Theology: A Reader*, Cassell 1998

Reader, John, *Local Theology*, SPCK 1994

Rowland, Chris and Vincent, John (eds), *Liberation Theology UK*, Urban Theology Unit 1995

Rowland, Chris and Vincent, John (eds), *Gospel from the City*, Urban Theology Unit 1997

Rowland, Chris and Vincent, John (eds), *Liberation Spirituality*, Urban Theology Unit 1999

Russell, Hilary, *Poverty Close to Home: The Political and Theological Challenge of Poverty in Britain*, Mowbray 1995

Sedgwick, Peter (ed), *God in the City: Essays and Reflections from the Archbishop of Canterbury's Urban Theology Group*, Mowbray 1995

Selby, Peter, *Grace and Mortgage*, Darton, Longman and Todd 1997

Smith, Austin, *Journeying with God: Paradigms of Power and Powerlessness*, Sheed and Ward 1990

Vincent, John, *Gospel in the 90s: A Theological Disputation*, Methodist Publishing House 1990

Vincent, John, *Radical Jesus: The Way of Jesus Then and Now*, Marshall Pickering 1986

Vincent, John (ed), *Stirrings: Essays Christian and Radical*, Epworth Press 1976

## (f) Periodicals

*ACT,* Ashram Community Trust, 178 Abbeyfield Road, Sheffield S4 7AY. Annual Booklet series

*Christian Community*, National Association of Christian Communities and Networks, Eton Road, Newport, NP9 0BL. Three times yearly

*City Cries*, Evangelical Coalition for Urban Mission, 70–74 City Road, London EC1Y 2BJ. Annual Journal on City Mission

*Crucible*, Board of Social Responsibility, Church House, Dean's Yard, London W1P 3NZ. Quarterly, on public policy issues

*CCWA Journal*, Churches' Community Work Alliance, 36 Sandygate, Wath-upon-Dearne, S63 7LW

*CCWA News*, Churches' Community Work Alliance, 36 Sandygate, Wath-upon-Dearne, S63 7LW

*Poverty,* Child Poverty Action Group (CPAG), 1–5 Bath Street, London EC1V. Three times yearly

*Urban Bulletin*, The Frontier Centre, 70–74 City Road, London EC1Y 2BJ. Bi-annual information bulletin on publications, training, conferences etc

# Key Gospel Passages

# General Index

# SICEM Branches

# SICEM People

(Single mentions in lists not included)